THE NATIONALIST MANIFESTO

By, Peter Vargus and Lana Weelhans

THE NATIONALIST MANIFESTO

PETER VARGUS & LANA WEELHANS

The Nationalist Manifesto (originally "The Foundations of the Nationalist Party") is a 2013 political pamphlet authored and published by the American couple Peter Vargus and Lana Weelhans. This independently distributed underground writing was widely circulated throughout the United States during the years leading up to the 2016 presidential election. The Manifesto is now recognized as the incendiary catalyst primarily responsible for the results of both the 2014 Congressional elections and the shocking events of the 2016 American presidential election.

Here now for the first time is the controversial manifesto which altered the fate of a nation, published fully intact in a formal, complete, and annotated edition with a new forward by its one surviving author. It presents a lucid analysis of the ongoing ideological warfare in modern day America and incites citizens to political action along national fault lines within education, technology, economics, and governance.

The Nationalist Manifesto distills Vargus and Weelhans' theories regarding how to sustain liberty and justice in a nation defined by rapid innovation, cultural diversity, and a lack of consensus authority. In their own words "Nationalists comprehend—the need for purpose, for culture, for faith, for a common vocabulary of moral and political right—the need for a moral and political right."

"The imitator knows
nothing worth mentioning
about what he imitates;
imitation is a kind of play and not serious…"

"…all nature ceases and becomes art."

"Indeed, it is a strange-disposed time:

but men may construe things after their fashion,

clean from the purpose of the things themselves."

"You are living a reality I left years ago. It quite nearly killed me."

Preface to the 2015 Edition:

The motivations behind this manifesto were clearly explained in the mission statement printed on our initial publication: to define and defend what it means to be an American. Contrary to the pomposity of the "citizens of the world", *this pursuit remains* the dominant theme of contemporary American life—the bipartisan national pastime is presently a shallow hypothesizing on the essence and character of America's past, present, and future. When conversing in crass generalizations, verity has little involvement. Broad phenomena resist tidy explanations; the clever rhetorician's goal is to posit "truth" in such a way as to seduce her listeners into accepting her vision. A beautiful phrasing or powerful aspiration can mold the national understanding of events, and *so the events themselves*, both as they happen and retroactively.

Mass distrust, anger, and a bipartisan sense of dread have their origin in widely shared delusions of insight and connectivity; modern information technologies ensure that no one is immune from believing they understand the unseen world. Yet, we are still human;

and so remain largely ignorant of matters beyond our immediate periphery—media channeled through multiple filters is more a perverse source of entertainment than any kind of illuminating information. To put it simply: no one knows how many "crazy people" are out there, or fully understands the motivations of their own hearts, let alone their neighbors'.

I do, however, think I understood Peter and his disappointment in the so-called educated classes of our society. *Most* of the well-credentialed are distinguished from the proverbial "unwashed masses" only by their cultivation of a *different set* of equally unmerited prejudices; not by advanced wisdom, or grace, or habits, or study, and especially not by any understanding of what makes our constitutional republic exceptional. Peter was disgusted by elites who, like so many aristocracies throughout history, make a virtue of scorning patriotism. Therein lies the germ of this entire manifesto: if you have *any smug condescension* towards our nation, you have no business occupying the halls of power in our democracy.

The challenge facing a work of thought, if it aspires to influence, is fundamentally a democratic one; for truth to carry weight it must be expressed in a manner that can be easily understood—in America *that which cannot be widely believed or practiced has no claim to legitimacy.* The impotent scholarly class has no music in their souls, no love for humanity, and no perspective beyond the pathetic nonsense of their unexceptional circles.[1] In reaching for a broader audience one must creatively blur the line between profundity and propaganda—*Art* may still possess the power to ensnare the people and guide their hopes. The artist is more courageous than the thinker in daring *not* to anatomize feeling to death—the artist presents "truth in the pleasant disguise of illusion"—the artist dares to be wrong.[2]

As the American public mind is suffering from a bout of temporary insanity, we, through this manifesto, *tried to grapple with*

[1]   "…the intellect, divine as it is…often, alas, acts the cannibal among the other faculties so that often, where the Mind is biggest, the Heart, the Senses, Magnanimity, Charity, Tolerance, Kindliness, and the rest of them scarcely have room to breathe." -*V. Woolf*

[2]   "I present the composition as an Art-Product alone: - let us say as a Romance; or, if I be not urging too lofty a claim, as a Poem. What I here propound is true: - * therefore it cannot die…Nevertheless it is as a Poem only that I wish this work to be judged after I am dead." -*E.A. Poe*

progressives on their own terms. If man is now to live *only* upon false and arbitrary convictions,[3] it still matters greatly which ideals he chooses and to what ends they lead. Our "best and brightest", plagued by boredom, stupidity, and selfishness, are no longer capable of supplying or becoming the citizen stones which construct the great edifice of a nation; they sooner drag the country down to their level.

It has been stressed by our adversaries that much of this manifesto is redundant of other works; of course it is! The answers to so many questions sit harmlessly on shelves, unable to strike at our present moment through the handful of people who still *engage* with them. Peter was unafraid to stand on the shoulders of giants; fear of repetition would have left Nietzsche admiring Callicles, Shakespeare studying Plutarch, and Plato quietly listening to Socrates. As the poet says "Each age, it is found, must write its own books; or rather, each generation for the next succeeding generation must write its own books." Peter once expressed his vision in an email conversation with me:

[3]   I reject this belief with all my heart and so did Peter.

"To aim for novelty is a childish pursuit, there is truly "nothing you can know that isn't known"; even the *power* and applications of new scientific discoveries are limited by what humans are willing to accept. No, any thinker seeking to impact his time should instead view himself as a conjurer of spirits, and, like a skilled litigator, summarize concepts and impressions in such a way as to guide his listeners inexorably to his desired conclusion. In this manner, we convoke and present established ideas in such a way as to lend support to our cause. The proper explanations for political phenomena are slippery; by bending them, or showing their most beneficent shades, we can ultimately influence or change both their core composition *and* how they are broadly understood.[4] We should be *timely* and unique in our expression so that we may excite the people into experiencing old wisdom anew or for the first time. Maybe great thinking is just a skillful rearrangement, or, at its height, a lonely mind writing love letters to fictions and longed for realities. Discontent *may* not always need to topple the status quo but

---

[4]   "It may well be that your true readers are not here as yet and that your books will cause them to materialize." -*S. Bellow*

9

rather can demand of it more thorough reckonings and convincing justifications. *We'll polemize for subtlety as norm/defining terms to dare them to conform.*"

As Peter's health began to decline he begged me to justify his suffering. Has any time period had to live with the knowledge that innovations could soon—but not quite soon enough—arrive which could have ended the anguish of today? Peter struggled against ever viewing his life as what he once called "a bad joke, the tensions of which, like most comedy, will be rendered stale by future change." He lamented how, despite his prior conviction that philosophy was a preparation for dying well, he was childishly unprepared; God's mercy felt absent, honor and duty were quick to flee, and hedonism is for the young. Only my love remained as a comfort. Nothing seems to be enough for anyone anymore... was it ever otherwise?

A thinker in crisis such as Peter will always have a difficult time proving to others, or to himself, that "circumstances really are dire and different this time." Stability is *always* falling apart, which is another way of saying things remain stable. I often told him that our present discord is caused more by the sloppy packaging of ideas than by any fundamental disagreements or dangers. Still, our crumbling republic merits at least an explanation, or a revitalizing platform, or a mere statement of the emotional pain felt at its passing.

Much has been said about our use of the word *Liberal*. I blame Peter's refusal to relinquish this term for the confusion surrounding our work, but as he told me "if we are brazen enough to try at restoring a nation we cannot shy away from restoring a definition." At this time I beg all readers to emancipate themselves from conventional idiocy.

His final question, which remains to be answered, articulates a simple wish: is it possible to reach and convince the vacuous but not yet lost progressives that their delusions have divided and damaged our nation while empowering the designs of a ruling class hell-bent on replacing citizen amity with a Hobbesian reorganization? All we have *to educate them*, within this manifesto, is the beauty of America seen through the eyes of youth, with the love of infant joy.

11

Relativists should be the first to agree "Beauty is truth, truth beauty, – that is all/ Ye know on earth, and all ye need to know".

What any writer chooses to emphasize depends in part upon the needs of her present moment; this manifesto represents *a moment* and our time's hope for the future. I have cleaned up Peters original citations and added a few explanatory notes of my own.

Lana Weelhans

November 7, 2015,

Philadelphia

Manifesto of The Nationalist Party

A specter is haunting American politics—the specter of Nationalism. All public actors stand opposed to this new movement: newsman and campus radical, bureaucrat and politician, "artist" and academic.

Is there any group who dares not decry the nationalist shame and does not knowingly distill its tenets into atavistic remnants of a brutal human past dominated by every bigotry ever given a name by some hackneyed PhD candidate? Is there any nationalist sentiment which is not immediately pruned from the realms of decency and cast as the worst of humanity bitterly clinging to a world now extinct?

Two things result from this fact:

1. Nationalism is despised by all "authorities" as a hate-filled threat.
2. Those who harbor nationalist tendencies deserve a higher class of explainer than the careerist mediocrities who spout nationalism's fury without representing its vision.

14

To this end, nationalists of America have gathered to sketch a program worth debating—an ethos which would the soul of nationalism if our centers of learning had not abandoned the goals of education.

Chapter 1: Progressive and Liberal

The future of all existing society is one of futilely defining man's nature.

Romantic and realist, bleeding-heart and conservative, global citizen and national, pluralist and tribalist stand in a perpetual state of opposition to each other on the social and political level and oftentimes within an individual person. As technology liberates man from numerous vestiges of the human condition these warring forces will be condensed further into two factions: creator vs created; malleable clay or a human animal.

Innovation alters anew the paradigms which govern humanity. The limits imposed by culture, sex, and genetics are constantly eroded opening up possibilities never before seen.

Such perpetual flux mandates ongoing revisions to the unquestioned assumptions behind a human life. Individuals, cultures, and governments hasten to adapt to a game whose rules are constantly changing. This struggle is felt nowhere more acutely than within the mind of a person deciding to accept or rebel against edicts which seem to have no permanent grounding—a new "reality" is always on the horizon.

Man is liberated from so much of what could have controlled him in previous epochs. He is made aware of the infinite variations of human life now available to him, yet, he experiences no corresponding increase in his power to escape the constraints upon his freedom which still remain. This tension—between near limitless choice and inescapable boundaries—creates political strife, and a spiritual searching for resolution which divides into two camps: the progressive and the liberal.

The disintegration of the family left a void in the identity development of the progressive. Mass communications and entertainment transitioned from background amusements to the forefront of perception. Programming tailored for consumption stepped into the vacuum and became the dominant form of moral education. Even strong families spent a mere fraction of time teaching each other when compared to the constant external stimuli.

The mapping of the genome and modern medicine removed the fantastical from the definition of "a person". All disciplines suffered a sense of inadequacy before the explanatory power of science and data. Every school of thought rushed to become more "scientific" in its method—forsaking their unique truths, the liberal arts became pale facsimiles of inquiry. Having abandoned what made their brand of wisdom appealing and revelatory, all spiritual truth was soon banished to the realm of homespun anachronism.

Meanwhile history's centuries long razing of all hierarchical authority elevated democratic values. The progressive cleared all vestiges of the republic's counter-majoritarian controls—the unsubtle will of man in a mass became the dominant force in the world. The progressive was both child and author of the new culture. The ever expanding branches of specialized knowledge replaced education with vocational training. The progressive may learn a niche skill, in all else it remains a barbarian.[5] Without the grounding of a strong family identity, religious values, or respect for national

---

[5]   "We shall have to say that he is a learned ignoramus, which is a very serious matter, as it implies that he is a person who is ignorant, not in the fashion of the ignorant man, but with all the petulance of one who is learned in his own special line." -*J.O. Gasset* (LW)

traditions and institutions, the progressive was left a hollow vessel, buffeted and led by the trends and superstitions of the crowd. Naturally, this new ethos met limits to its power with contempt—the force of mass agitation admitted no rival as all former sources of guidance were supplanted and dismissed as outdated relics.

Telecommunications molded social reality through the vehicles of peer pressure, oversimplification, and constant bombardment. Capitalism, freed from ethical restraint, packaged morality; the highest selling products were those which flattered the vanity of the progressive.

News media and all public "arts" entertainment were designed consciously and unconsciously to satisfy their purchasers' most exploitable impulses. The market happily produced the desired products and, like children offered candy instead of nourishment, generations rushed to be molded by values corrupted in nature by consumerism. There is now no counter-culture—businessman and revolutionary alike parrot marketing campaigns developed in boardrooms. Three feelings predictably emerged as the highest selling flavors: the individual is born perfect and needs no tutelage;

this truth applied to the individual must in turn apply equally to all people; the generation which fully "lives" these truths possesses a wisdom which transcends all of human history.

As the ranks of the progressive grew it came to dominate the mechanisms which had led to its creation thereby accelerating its rise. What was once merely profit exploitation took on a fanatical zeal as the progressive disseminated its code with prolific effect; its values pervade all entertainment, political debate, and educational institutions. The progressive is both buyer and seller, advertiser and product.

The progressive, sculptor and creation, has remade the world in its image.

The progressive has waged war against culture; it has rendered judgment upon human history. It has recast all civilization as violence—the progressive does not value ethical ideals, rather it sees only the surface inequalities which result from their application. It perverts observational science by selectively proving its own presuppositions—it believes only in obvious data and dismisses all unquantifiable wisdom. The progressive lacks subtlety and explains phenomena through the lens of power: a social contract rewards and punishes its adherents based on its organizing principles; the progressive cannot abide winners or losers—it reinterprets "society" as *brutality* which dominates the vulnerable.[6]

The progressive strives to prove the arbitrary nature of codes of conduct. It believes that people have always mistaken mere circumstantial pressures for eternal mandates; fleeting accidents are its *sole* explanation for every form of human morality. The progressive calls *necessity* a temporal mirage—the needs of today have no right to constrain it; society fails by giving weight to outmoded scarcities and past paradigms. The progressive admits of no limiting principle to the right of self-expression and discovery.[7]

The progressive has debased and augmented the role of government as defender of natural rights. Governance now exists to prevent all

[6] The progressive unoriginally asserts that what a polity calls *Justice* has always ever been a lie by which "the ruling group sets down laws for its own advantage," and with destructive glee cackles that "one fact is common to all past ages, *viz.,* the exploitation of one part of society by the other." *Thrasymachus~K. Marx* (LW)

[7] The Progressive lacks the canonical mastery and sense of humor needed to seriously assert that *"there are altogether no moral facts... [or that]* Morality is merely an interpretation of certain phenomena—more precisely a misinterpretation." *-F. Nietzsche* (LW)

community or cultural repression of the progressive's supreme entitlement: the onanistic esteem of self. Where political movements once marched for all peoples to be judged by the content of their character, the progressive attacks *the concepts of character and judgment* as the root causes of past injustice.

The progressive cannot command society without constantly conjuring past enemies of decency. There is no eradicated villain or children's bogeyman the progressive does not reanimate to stalk its civilization. All the phobias and *all the -isms* can never cease to exist; for as they ebb the progressive battles them always more ferociously. It maintains its dominion by thwarting its victory—its zeal revives anew the masses' waned bigotries and hurls their sensibilities back in time. It must continuously denigrate the heroes of man's past and erect new idols. All leaders, intellectuals, and warriors of history become irredeemable victimizers; its own champions too are quickly torn down as it constantly discovers new oppressions of which it retroactively accuses its forebears.

The progressive rules by way of this perpetual struggle. It represses any dreams of life beyond grappling with the ever-increasing phantoms of the past.

The progressive has destroyed faith in practical judgment. It scours the globe for every human type to display. This is not done from empathy—it fetishizes "the other" as demonstrative of randomness. In this pursuit it classifies people into the most basic identity groups. It offers these reductive creations a condescending drug of shallow solidarity and aggrievement in opposition toward a fictitious majority. But there is of course no majority; due to this manipulation, society has fractured into small clans, all of whom feel ostracized by a homogenous oppressor. The progressive asserts that group disagreement proves all values are arbitrary. Therefore, no order deserves primacy or power. It is the progressive who in this balancing seizes all control, for it alone claims freedom from the bias of balkanized group membership. It misrepresents itself as protector and savior—the progressive is the secret oppressor majority![8]

[8] "The mode is to seek to become trusted by the [nation] that is disunited, and to manage oneself between the parties as an arbiter until they come to [strife]. When they do come to [strife], it is to give favors slowly to the weaker party, both to keep them at war longer and make them [the nation] consume themselves..." -*N. Machiavelli* (LW)

Believing in no escape from the sway of tribal identity, the individual comes to assume that its judgment is a circumstantial accident, the expression of which is a form of oppression.

The progressive has created a social fabric of cookie-cutter cosmopolitans, a diversity of superficial decorations. It is "courageously" an oppressed -, an autonomous -, a normal -, an observant -, a liberated -. There is, however, nothing behind the curtain—the progressive does not read the philosophy of its assigned identity, it is not enflamed by the poetry of its forerunners; its foundational tenets of consumable plastic popular "culture" admit none of the tensions and depth which animated the originals.

The progressive loves quaint variations and dull vestiges; exotic food, bizarre ancestors, and novel clothing are titillating, some people even celebrate different holidays! It does not tolerate vitality; nuance which pierces the surface risks passion—so dogmatism—so imposition. Culture is best served chilled by a limp arm's length ambivalence towards itself. Progressive society members are one— united by boring simplicity, lazy indignation, and the childish desire to be special but not unique.

The progressive meets those with hope for deeper purpose, for meaning, and for adherence to values as a kindly veterinarian. From a young age it was dosed and now prescribes an intravenous drip of sensory overload—into every vein pumps a steady stream of alcohol, television, designer drugs both illicit and pharmaceutical, gilded toys, pornography, and *social consciousness*. The machinery is effective. The populace is kept docile; the medication switches off agitation, longing, and dynamism. The chemical dials turn on a numb stasis which imagines a brotherhood of man through a pleasant haze.

The progressive has banished the potential abuses of citizen engagement and its correctable mistakes; the iron cage of bureaucratization removes this dirtiness from politics.[9] It preserves the appearance of a republic—with a rotted heart. Elections are a sporting event, they enflame some passions and conjure fun amusements for the masses, but the outcome is irrelevant. The

---

[9] No American should accept or desire that "… as a result of technical and economic developments, the legal ignorance of the layman will increase…and hence [laws] character as a specialists' domain. Inevitably the notion must expand that the law is a rational technical apparatus, which is continuously transformable in the light of expediential considerations and devoid of all sacredness of content." -*M. Weber* (LW)

progressive administrative apparatus is unchanged no matter which wrestler takes the belt. The fervor of entertainment media enhances the façade as gravity and subtlety are kept out of the public forum; complex issues are resolved layers removed from civic debate or concern.

We see then the progressive swallowing up, digesting, and distilling old forms to serve as its mouthpieces. As a Christian, a logician, a republican, a democrat, or a patriot, it is in costume—it is *always solely a progressive*, melding and hollowing phrases to *that* ideal. Its "religion" tolerates all spirituality but no dogma; its "education" conjures perspectives but claims to teach no wisdom. This lack of linguistic precision is no mystery—as politics corrupts individuals it too corrupts language.[10] As so much of human identity is now experienced digitally, projecting a virtue trumps *living* it. The avatar of an ideal is more "real" than the physical form. The progressive

---

[10] "The word *Fascism* has now no meaning except in so far as it signifies 'something not desirable'... Since you don't know what Fascism is, how can you struggle against Fascism? One need not swallow such absurdities as this, but one ought to recognize that the present political chaos is connected with the decay of language, and that one can probably bring about some improvement by starting at the verbal end." -*G. Orwell*

holy men and tyrants are not defined by deeds or body count but by the degree to which they exhibit—the progressive aesthetic.

All principles and faiths, despite their choice of doublespeak theatricality, have unknowingly converted to progressivism and offer their power only to the progressive cause.

A simultaneous movement now undermines progressive society, presenting a final hurdle to its dominion. Globalism and revolutions in technological efficiencies are challenging capitalism's promise of *creative* destruction. The progressive *is so certain* that, unlike in previous eras of disrupt and class realignments, the capacity and labor of ever more subsets of people have been rendered *permanently obsolete*; the horizons of artificial intelligences ensure fewer and fewer individuals are needed for even the most massive undertakings. Where once the market guided an outdated craftsman to join a new guild or pioneer a novel service, today's candlestick maker finds a *self-sufficient machine* making lightbulbs—installed and delivered electronically. A handful of extreme outliers—in capacity, drive or invention, birthright connections, or unique physical gifts—along with the political and entertainment class, still have something to trade. A few professionals augmented by computers can surpass the output and wealth of nations.

As capitalism has given a universal flavor to cities, this new "Meritocrat" has no need for or allegiance to its country of accidental origin. It knows no fellowship or community neighbors; this new elite has a global playground. Its materialism organically allies it to progressivism as both a perfunctory adherent and a manipulator. It holds the ever growing rabble in contempt for their illogical beliefs, vicious responses to scarcity, and primitive loyalties. It constructs for them a welfare state as a kind of serf protection fee—they are kept fed; the meritocrat merely asks them not to make a fuss. *But…* the mass has imbibed too much of the progressive's lessons. The streets are not lined with young Socratics craving rigor or symposium; with no meaning to pursue, the individual gnashes its teeth in frustration and longing. Despair and oblivion are a common result. The rest, with no remedy for spiritual pain, turn to material envy; progressivism teaches that the prosperity and influence of the meritocrat is unearned and unfairly bestowed. The ever-present media, internet, and cultural worship of wealth ensures that envy leads to rage as the individual finds a *new need for itself*: the masses of humanity threaten to tear apart the progressive order.

The meritocrat responds with hostility, not introspection. Its innovations are no longer small steps for man, it seeks to overleap mankind. The logical final solution to which progressive hostilities and dogmas trend is revealed as the extinction of homo-sapiens and all the pointless Cro-Magnon bickering and allegiances—the violence of race, religion, philosophy, family, politics, nations, and always the whining need for purpose and eating. If the creature's imperfections make it incompatible with progressive coding, after so much failed reprogramming, the progressive will junk the hardware. Man 2.0 will be more content and adaptable—more able to run the progressive operating system without the silly bugs—a genetic perfection or cyborg...then inorganic wonder...and self-updating! The human animal is far weaker, far more destructive, and far too prone to error. It jeopardizes the mission; the cargo must be jettisoned.[11]

---

[11] "Dave, this conversation can serve no purpose anymore. Goodbye." -*S. Kubrick*

The progressive starts to work towards its own obsolescence and the way humanity ends—not with a bang but with an upload.

As the progressive imagines a sophisticated eugenics, or merger then replacement with machines, its back is exposed to the species which refuses any future of which man is not a part—the liberal.

As the progressive seeks to leave man's frailties behind, so too does the liberal, the American Cartesian, begin to stir—a class of romantics, who insist upon their definition of what *is* a human being. Subject to years of vivisection at the hands of the progressive apparatus, these individuals emerge scarred but stubborn in their vision.[12]

Behold the liberal in its new-born blisses—the warmth of a parental home and so much familiarity—a community of similar hopes, guided by matching fears and needs. Too soon its trusted idols— parental wisdom, citizenship, religion, and the culture by which it

[12] "To escape from the spirit of system, from the yoke of habits, from family maxims, from class opinions, and, up to a certain point, from national prejudices; to take tradition only as information, and current facts only as a useful study for doing otherwise and better; to seek the reason for things by themselves and in themselves alone, to strive for a result without letting themselves be chained to the means, and to see through the form to the foundation: these are the principal features that characterize what I shall call the philosophic method of the Americans." -A. *Tocqueville* (LW)

defines itself—are touched with a hammer. Like countless generations before, it blinks into adulthood. Progressive society does not guide this transformation to a fruitful end; it offers distractions in place of discovery. The liberal is thrown backwards into a prolonged adolescence of empty sensuality and juvenile posturing.

Progressivism has converted the goal of education from development to regression. The liberal's inner voice of reason becomes an exasperated translator of a duplicitous tongue. A progressive teaches, "the injustices of history must never be repeated," but it means "present injustice eases present guilt"; it proclaims "one must consider various perspectives," it means "to dissent is to be a fanatic"; it says "inequalities of power and wealth are unjust" to assert "personal choices deserve no consequence"; it affirms "authority is valid only if, by consent, it serves justice and liberty" to declare "there is no God but the bureaucrat, and the ivy league sociologist is his prophet". After being "taught" hypocrisy and that *logic is always prejudiced*, the liberal has permission to embrace its favorite versions. It returns to the preferences of its childhood—not

31

from a primal sympathy or philosophic mind, but as a defense against madness.

Progressive education offers no tools for self-liberation or the development of reason. Bruised, the liberal reverts to its youthful state without the accompanying sense of inquisitiveness.

The progressive mechanisms admit no rival; the liberal must succumb or risk this stubborn infancy.

Beyond the university and away from the corporate pipelines or government hierarchies of the meritocrat, all learn and become teachers of liberalism. Pontification on imaginary half-truths gives way to the wisdom of practical experiences. Small business, local administration, the *innate* preferences of young children, relationship dynamics and their predictable resolutions, policy intentions and the *results* of intrusive designs…, hasten one's conversion to liberalism. *Living* elucidates the non-negotiable imperatives for which so many mothballed virtues account.

The liberal confronts progressivism's consequences—promises of increased wages and dignified labor delivered as tax hikes or emasculating dependencies; the "impartial" correction of "bias" creating a patronage system of entrenched corruption from municipality to capital; the exhibitionist celebration of the downtrodden *sowing feelings of inadequacy and otherwise unfelt oppression* in the newly scarred souls of protected classes; and a "social planning" incompatible with cultural prerogatives. The liberal laughs at the ogre club of spurious statistics and meaningless correlations; alleged gender disparities and cultures' disparate advancements have easier explanations than progressive banalities. Beset by accusations of hateful intent, with full knowledge that the distant progressive views it as a mere number in an equation, the liberal responds that perverse incentives create unforeseen consequences. The only "privilege" is to know you are loved and doing your duty; and corpses cannot be made more or less dead, their sufferings alleviated by present aesthetics.

The liberal movement begins as a disjointed cluster of many concerns united in their sense of progressive rot. Like animals in captivity which harm themselves in agitation the liberal mass lashes out at the mere *symptoms* of progressivism—an administrator shreds constitutional design and sparks the collective *against government itself*; the vibrant culture that welcomed immigrants to *join in its expression*, in decay sees an invading army clearing out hostile natives; rage directed towards the disappearing difference between insight and mental illness prompts *rejection of fluidity and reflection*. The liberal does not see the root enemy who has poisoned so many benign ideals—*the progressive* advances with each pyrrhic liberal victory over poorly chosen targets!

The liberal begins to comprehend its situation—the super-machinery of global trade, efficient mechanization, and federalized forces of government exert power beyond the control of any political process. Points of no return have been reached.[13] All discussion of which

---

[13] "…the peaceful and constructive use of worldwide technological power, a use in which all of us collaborate as captive beneficiaries through rising production, consumption, and sheer population growth…the net total of these threats is the overtaxing of nature, environmental and (perhaps) human as well. Thresholds may be reached in one direction or another…where processes initiated by us will run away from us on their own momentum—and toward disaster." -*H. Jonas*

dorm-room buzzword best serves justice must account for the dependency of entire cities on the seamless operation of markets for food and water. The liberal distills an *identity which can endure and direct these forces* from fragments ignored by progressivism: love for America, self-reliance, religiosity, and constitutionalism. It sees moral worthiness as the sole right to power; it watches free markets surpass the designs of planners; it respects founding law as timeless justice not an evolving tool. Conflicts with progressives mirror rival nations barking indecipherable bile at each other; confronted with progressive longings for a system to negate human action, the liberal seeks to prosper *according to* human nature—no perfect clockwork—*the perfectibility of man*.[14] When faced with a dueling concept of "history's arch" the progressive often resorts to violence and repression.

The liberal resists the forms of masturbation favored by progressives; it does not evangelize so called national trends or make

---

[14] "We assert…that happiness is the actualization and complete practice of virtue…a city is excellent, at any rate, by its citizens'—those sharing in the regime—being excellent; and in our case all the citizens share in the regime…Now even if it is possible for all to be excellent but not each of the citizens individually, the latter is more choiceworthy; for all [being excellent] follows from [all] individually [being excellent]." -*Aristotle*

sweeping judgments of causal and historical relationships—through the interworking of municipalities and community activism it learns judgment and practices justice and *equality before the law*. Minute differences of race or custom are of no concern—the liberal sees its cause expressed across a diverse range of beliefs. It has yet to encounter a people who do not honor familial love, struggle to provide for children, wonder at life's gifts, fear death, and hate taxes. Its citizens unite to leave behind the darkness of the old world's violent jealousies and sectarian hate. The liberal preserves a nation liberated from the shackles of history, guided by universal enlightenment. [15]

Liberals are wary of progressive gifts—they hear the denouncing of "insurmountable obstacles" as a clandestine attempt to possess and cripple entire subsets of the people. The progressive reserves special viciousness for individuals it views as its rightful slaves who dare to leave the farm. The liberal affirms—we are just one race here. *It is American.*

[15] "Citizens, by birth or choice, of a common country, that country has a right to concentrate your affections. The name of American, which belongs to you in your national capacity, must always exalt the just pride of patriotism more than any appellation derived from local discriminations." -*G. Washington*

The progressive subverts civic unity with a sinister social engineering: it destroys primary education. Forced into impotent incubation at prolonged day care, the ambitious liberal is then hindered by a litany of newly created unnecessary degrees and certifications. By coddling away primary skills and training, the progressive left the liberal helpless—it must tithe for a hollow passport. Federal "aid" and regulation skyrocket costs ensuring fealty to progressive institutions—the nurse, doctor, and general counsel are indentured servants to the hospital, not autonomous community pillars.

Accepting the progressive grip on advancement, liberals quarrel with each other. Programs to elevate subsets of the population have instead degraded society and turned potential allies to suspicion and resentment. Preferring the superficial picturesque to the brutal generational struggle of empowerment, the progressive gives the appearance of equal dignity not the capabilities to define it oneself. No liberal battles this machine; they argue control of its fringe quotas or prices.

The progressive's perfecting system—the gorgeous centralizations, the cloud-capped world trade organizations, the solemn consumer finance protections, the great federal bureaucracy itself[16]—prays for *an ultimate apparatus* to remove the imperatives of life. The liberal too seeks a form of liberation. Seeing always in man's mind the power to construct a heaven of hell or hell of heaven, it works to *elevate the spirit and capability of the individual person*. No matter the evolution of progressive choice architecture or gilded prisons, the liberal *knows* man carries suffering and need *within*—but also great potential and civilization; it rejects any naïve master equation for human thriving through safe space design.

It dawns on the progressive that it is a failed experiment; the attempted removal of *all* human restrictions instead gives rise to *new mandates*. As cells organize into tissue which clusters into the appendages which in turn make up organisms—*"life" is a struggle against entropy*. None can practice a dada politics;[17] the erasure of

---

[16] "…shall dissolve/And, like this insubstantial pageant faded,/Leave not a rack behind" -*W. Shakespeare*

[17] Dadaism was an avant-garde art movement for which Peter had great affinity. It was spawned in part as a reaction to the madness of World War. It is defined by the illogical, by nonsense, and by freeform protest against the ordered systems of reason and culture which demonstrably led to the pointless

traditional understandings *is always a midpoint*—soon replaced by another taste and way of bringing order to chaos.

Tortured into feigning an ideal not meant for humans the progressive in conflict becomes a hybrid of the worst of both types: an uncritical dogmatist against human nature. Progressivism's loudest advocates today call their unchanging vision... eternal truth. Despite the openness rhetoric of progressivism, this *mutilated liberal germ* is its primary offspring; even the most species-life conscious progressive *imposes limiting principles* guided by its own bizarre definition of humanity.[18]

By perceiving tyranny in all forms of constraint, the progressive can only suffer pointlessly as a slave—man is never wholly free from arbitrary controls; inequalities of health, luck, spouses, or genetic gifts cannot be marched against or legislated away as long as

and brutal slaughter of millions. An example of a Dadaist Bill of Rights is summarized thusly: plarkinfal klingoh deletibino wah wah naxcocine teleckmo jeedev jeeqiop lamanata polifgaz shuuunda sundito kalaxapy maf maf delgabeev. (LW)

[18] For a more thorough explanation of the term "species-life conscious" and other communist literature, see Peter Vargus "Misunderstanding Oneself: Marx Properly Read as a Romantic Poet of *Feelings Masquerading as Thoughts;* Taking the Passionate Hyperbole of Young Men Seriously as A Recipe for Mass Murder" Published in the Franz Kafka Society Journal of Artistic Types Desperate to Escape the Legal Profession (LW).

humans exist. The liberal blesses *inescapable adversity* as life not injustice: the legitimacy of power and anguish—and existence itself—needs poetry not sophistry.

Endless information and surfeit awareness beyond the limits of what an animal can process—too much of history, current events, and ideology—breeds paralysis not wisdom. *Innately unable* to live by a chaos theory of social understanding, both types cry out for narrative purpose, faith, and wonder.

Natural mandates pressure communities as they do individuals; living with diversity demands a measure of commonality or sparks civil war; to dwell together is to treat alike. The liberal embraces the reality of physical space; a nation still *imposes cultural and economic unity* despite progressive delusions of global citizenship.

The liberal will call its homeland home. Love of country is love of common purpose, common values, and familiarity; love necessarily expresses a preference which excludes. It *welcomes* revision; *true love* means discord, passion, and compromise—loves not love that replaces intimacy with respectful fear. It wants dissent, forgiveness, but above all else bonding. While the progressive attempts to halt all cultural destruction or growth by freezing the world in time, the liberal understands that to live a single day is to hazard every facet of oneself. Circumstantial accidents and so many interactions daily alter the fabric of individuals and entire cultures. Transformation is inevitable; it can be natural—or twisted by progressive tampering. Liberalism is a free people risking the discord and experiments of diverse love, rejecting disparate isolation and hateful distrust under the spineless thumb of a bureaucrat or computer.

The liberal apportions national and global *activism* small care, not from lack of empathy, but because that which it is *forever incapable of understanding* should not command its full heart. Like water turned to mud sliding downhill, information is corrupted and truth dirtied in transit; we can only ever be aware of distant affairs through a triply obscured lens.[19] Liberals humbly accept that this unavoidable ignorance in action often magnifies harms despite intent. The liberal distrusts the limited expert who posits broad explanations of complex events—somewhere there is a cabal of tax attorneys, or

---

[19] "Rumour is a pipe/Blown by surmises, jealousies, conjectures" -*W. Shakespeare*

municipal zoning officers, algorithmic programmers, primatologists, or mathematician dentists who claim worldwide understandings. The liberal penetrates this murkiness by caring for and affecting what it can honestly perceive: justice in its own polity resonant with its country's great notion.

The liberal admits no impediments to the *idea of America*.[20] Unique in all history it is a people united by vision and right rather than superficial features—by soul not sign—the one truly modern towering creation of all ages of humanity. *The American is the **beginning** of the human future* not a bridge to something higher. The progressive, a dying animal that knows not *why* it is, courts enfeeblement while the liberal gives an ever-fixed mark—the shining city of love and tolerance, which ended fascism and fights oppression, which empowered millions to *raise themselves* out of poverty and strife, which welcomes the world to freely share in the glory and the dream, the civic community guided by the light from above—the autonomous child of law and philosophy which lifts the

---

[20] "It is the star to every wand'ring bark,/Whose worth's unknown, although his height be taken" -*W. Shakespeare*

lamp beside the golden door will shake off the cynical progressive regime!

In summarizing the awakening of the liberal, we described the battle over how to define mankind and its chosen destiny up to the point where progressivism's secret hatred for humanity causes it to devour itself allowing an American nationalism to guide the nation.

The immediate future of all society will strive to answer two questions: what is a human being and toward what goals should our species aspire? No answers can avoid imposing themselves upon every level of political action and social order. Any creed must provide inspiration which allows for humans to prosper in adherence. Where previous codes served man as the measure of their success, progressivism chips away at every facet of human existence. The liberal is reduced to a plaything—stifled and rejected in all hopes, its desires and essence mere glitches its rulers long to erase. It becomes clear that the progressive can no longer control society. It suffocates and leaves behind the highest needs of the people; the ruling meritocrat looks upon all that man is with contempt and cannibalizes its subjects. No creature can cheerfully work towards obliteration; progressivism fails to convey why humanity should continue digging its own grave, with no reason for suffering, hating its nature.

Progressivism must continuously convince society of its own unworthiness; fear and contempt lead to a desire to shed the human core and live as new creatures. However, progressivism has abandoned mankind in spirit before capable of leaving it in body. Rejecting *all* limitations has led to rage and despair. Progressivism has destabilized itself by teaching an ideal hostile to humanity; it cannot explain why it should exist any longer—its decline, and America's salvation walk hand in hand with the victory of liberalism.

Chapter II. Liberals and Nationalists

What role do the nationalists play in the liberal future?

They embody the *highest* expression of liberalism's response to the demands of our time.

They provide a governing center for the liberals' ambitions—a guiding precept around which variant strains of liberalism must organize.

Nationalism is an outgrowth of the inescapable legacy of progressivism led by the better angels of a liberal nature.

Nationalists differ from other respondents to today's American schism in the following ways: 1. They accept that the emetic dogma of progressivism cannot be swiftly purged from the national consciousness; they do battle within the world of its creation. 2. They, in quarrels between liberals and progressives, see through to the core antagonistic principles and seek to unite both factions in a common expression of the nationalist cause.

The immediate aim of the nationalists is to seize both parties; to make the progressive see its own destructive consequences; to elevate the liberal to the centers of power and political discourse; to topple the institutionalized mistakes of progressivism.

As Lincoln transformed a confederated union with a new birth of a *new nation*—as emergence from The Depression forever altered the citizen's relationship to its government—nationalists do not advocate the return to a superseded ideal, inadequate to the problems of its time. A living organism should not question whether its attributes are the *best* answers to the problems of survival—the success of its evolution is shown by its continued existence.

Nationalists do not long for imagined simplicities of the past; they are not burning antibiotics or tending victory gardens for sustenance.

But, an interconnected globe is no excuse for American leaders to ignore American interests. Nationalists approach a more perfect union *with their essence, their family, and their country*, at its center.

Nationalism is the unifying principle possible for America today; like an indecisive youth swept by time to an unchosen future, the nation—the world—*will be directed* and changed in ways both anticipated and undesired. Nationalism is the least harmful chance to galvanize a diverse people to a greater happiness and peace.

Nationalists comprehend—the need for purpose, for culture, for faith, for a common vocabulary of moral and political right—the need for a moral and political right. Theirs is the only ideal large enough to contain the multitudes and contradictions of American aspirations.

Nationalists equate human endeavor with jazz music; creation, improvisation, and free self-expression are made possible by a structured underlying theme; *no society* means no art, no justice, no science, and no progress.

47

Nationalists force their country's leadership to take their eyes off grander illusions and masturbatory indulgences; the rulers of a society should have more in common with their own people than with the elite classes of foreign lands.

From these understandings, the theory of nationalism can be summarized in a single statement: For a country to survive and prosper, a unitary purpose must guide all other hopes, arguments, and perceptions of reality; American exceptionalism—a republic and new-Eden ideal—is the one remaining self-evident truth.

We nationalists have been accused of an ideology which ignores facts, reason, and tolerance—the foundation, we are told, of what it means to be just and American.

Dispassionate reasoning free from implicit bias? Inquiry which aims at *wisdom*? Do you mean a universal brotherhood with shared hopes for the future? Progressivism rejects these forms of curiosity and solidarity; it calls such ambitions callow ignorance or thinly veiled hatred of different perspectives.

Or do you mean progressive reasoning and its "tolerant" love for perspectives?

Do we call ourselves blind because the eye cannot see the infrared spectrum? Progressives deride "judgment" as *fully* tainted by identity interest, equating incompleteness with worthlessness. Yet, decisions must still be made with and despite man's limited lens.[21] Awareness of our dependence on partial filters blesses liberal actions with humility; it makes progressives call all reasoning, but their own, corrupted.

Progressivism has created an arms race between resentment and centralized power. Its social engineering on behalf of one faction enrages and disempowers those ignored. To salvage tranquility, progressives commit further abuse, now on behalf of the newly-

---

[21] "Deconstruction is fun. It is also quite useless for those who want to get on with the business of living and acting in the real world." -*A. Scalia*

incensed and forgotten, thus enflaming the impotent masses further. This escalating domination and hostility will end explosively if not redeemed by a universal identity and a single garment of destiny. The rejection of *any* common laws of agreement has not increased justice; it has neutered prudence and enabled the progressive's terrible resolve for political control.

This faux godlike apprehension is made shallow by failing to wrestle with the contradictions, shortcomings, *and virtues* inherent in every social order or ethical tradition; "central precepts are *never* impartial, therefore every regime is built *solely* upon lies and violence" brays the progressive.

Progressivism has destroyed the *legitimacy* of Power but not the *existence* of Power. Poisoning a people's hope and ability to govern does not end government; it relocates decision-making. A lack of fellowship or common social practice leads to federal domination to protect against brutality.

What becomes of "neutral truth"? The more divided a people the greater the distance between knowledge and its universal acceptance. A "fact" is objective; its power—its applications, its usefulness—depends first on civic trust. Culture war ends communal integrity thus degrading all science; "truth" becomes unknown and unknowable. The people grow like savages, accepting only observations which aid political purposes.[22]

In this climate, the liberal's only hope is that a person of similar concerns *might direct* the countless levers of governmental discretion insulated from democratic process. With no influence, and no understanding of the legal forces which saturate its life, it votes with the vain wish that a shared set of familiar beliefs will guide the invisible administrator.

And the clown mouthpieces of the "educated" rabble call that stupidity. A nation of helpless sharecroppers voting purely to express identity frustrations is the *height* of the progressive ideal. The people

---

[22] "Even so our houses and ourselves and children/Have lost, or do not learn for want of time,/The sciences that should become our country…" -*W. Shakespeare*

have no real sway and are degraded to such a state that they deserve none.

Unless! Unless a shared sense of wonder can enable civic vitality by transcending strife. Man's greatest challenges lack clear resolutions: can a *truly diverse* people, through *self-government,* preserve a shared justice, liberty, and autonomy…can the millions be raised in awareness or is a future of soft despotism inevitable and desirable…what rights are too sacred to risk in popular sovereignty and who decides that question…what is innate and what *should* be fostered within the piece of work that is man? The nationalist understands what is at stake should "America" fail.[23] It feels itself too mighty to aim small; it has chosen optimism; it has chosen unity; it has chosen a surfeit of awe; it has chosen freedom; it has chosen a republic; it has chosen a constitution; it has chosen enlightenment.

---

[23] "…it seems to have been reserved to the people of this country, by their conduct and example, to decide the important question, whether societies of men are really capable or not of establishing good government from reflection and choice, or whether they are forever destined to depend for their political constitutions on accident and force." -*A. Hamilton*

Progressives call these acknowledgments radical or anachronistic. *American* nationalism is the only *forward-thinking* movement; it alone seeks to answer the *open* questions of the present and global future.

Immediately the cries are heard: all must have a say! You have no right to ignore the international order! Fools—there is no such thing. The triumphs of human rights, prosperity, rule of law, and relative global tranquility are the legacy and gifts of American supremacy.

Nationalists demand the world help bear the cost of beating back savagery. We will not abide a foreign policy of naïveté or appeasement, but we no longer welcome the thankless task of propping up dying civilizations; we care about American interests and American lives.

"But we must remedy inequality at home and abroad," echoes the hackneyed refrain. Nationalists agree, this is the gravest modern issue; those destitute of a *rigorous* education, a thriving family, a moral tradition, or a love of liberty's processes—forever bereft of purpose, critical thinking, or spiritual depth—are doomed as chattel to whatever flavor of autocracy is in vogue.

The thriving classes know this, yet abdicate their most basic civic duty: they who live conducive to joy and prosperity owe more than a silent example; they owe their voices and their guidance. The meritocrat has abandoned all responsibility; it makes the obligatory statements and donations but refuses to be its brothers' keeper. Despite its own strict code of conduct, it is unwilling to risk scorn by silencing the preachers of bacchanalian shamelessness. The nationalist does more than just nudge;[24] *it leads; it teaches.*

Or did you mean material inequality? The opioid of righteous indignation by which you keep the masses in misery and subservience. Spend a minute navigating a labyrinthine corporate structure, a tax schedule, or any number of savings vehicles. See what the highly sophisticated and well-advised wealthy, who now

---

[24] Behavioral economics and choice architecture show great promise. Yet, they sometimes offer fascinating ways for cowardly minds to avoid preaching morality. If it is sound policy to automatically enroll workers into retirement savings accounts, thereby increasing the use of such tools of prosperity, one would think it is morally right—or morally mandatory—to preach thrift and saving as virtues. (LW)

have the entire world in which to structure their holdings, do to your fantasy.

"We can raise tax rates!" To bar new additions to the then-made permanent aristocracy? "Coupled with estate taxes!" And innovations in evasive transactions, asinine restructurings, and novel citizenship changes? "Take over the entire financial sector!" Strangle 99% of the populations' access to credit or investment while the shrewd migrate to private markets and alternative asset classes? "Corporations must pay their fair share!" A corporation is a piece of paper.

Nationalists tire of the millionaire political class venting its hostilities towards the centimillionaire class; your bickering over the corporate monoliths and wealth concentrations *your misguided regulation helped create* does nothing to aid those who lack your marketability and the luxury of your petty jealousies. This smokescreen masks the important inequalities which plague us—in family composition, in lucrative skill acquisition, in exposure to honest discourse, in the fostering of philosophic minds.

55

"So you would have us all slaves to the vicissitudes of an unfeeling market" bleat the progressives. Nationalists have no such economic religiosity. They care about objectives; regulatory distortions or destructive measures are easily justified if the wealth sacrificed is repaid in some other type of currency—be it increased public health, civic cohesion, safety, or moral values. Society *can* be organized in any manner but to what end?

Nationalists beg for honesty and a vision. Is "middle class" a salary statistic? a comparison? a mindset or lifestyle expectation? or access to services? or unsubsidized self-realization? What is the social price of redistributionist schemes in bloated inefficiency, psychological detriment, resentments, and future generations' dreams? Stubbornness and pandering assail the nationalists' ears. In talk of automation, global labor competition, and regulation the economic dogmatists and moral polemicists lack a common unit of value: they speak past each other. Nationalists know that progressivism has long hated free enterprise, hated personal responsibility, and hated

American cultural ambitions; they tentatively trust in the liberals' stated goals.

"But you nationalists are violent and vicious" wails the progressive.

The blended composition of *American* nationalism insulates us against mimicking the horrific errors of lesser nations who have expressed jingoistic sentiments. Nationalists vote, they organize communities, and use gentle persuasion to welcome others to their cause; progressives riot, jam highways, bully opposition, destroy property, and brutalize dissidents.

"But we must make restitution for the horrors of history!" New technology and understandings constantly rewrite what it means to suffer or ignore oppression; *not what it meant.*[25] As you cannot feel the imperatives of the future, you cannot fully comprehend the past. The hardest thing for any time period to forgive is its predecessors' lack of access to present solutions or priorities. Future man will have

---

[25] See Lana Weelhans; <u>Women Before and After the Birth Control Pill; Two Different Species, Two Different Definitions of Justice.</u> (LW)

no empathy for your inability to teleport, your taste for meat, your limited global stability, or the constraints imposed by your need to constantly work to survive; you will one day be held responsible for ongoing genocides and the extinctions of countless species.

You are an equal legacy of the past's errors and triumphs; each individual finds the faults and genius of all persons in all time periods *within*.[26] Nationalists meld oppressor and oppressed alike as a shared heritage. We are untranslatable to the progressive's divisive categorizations;[27] we are the civil rights movement, the immigrant hopeful, *and* the fearful who stood in the doorway; we *choose and become the best* of America, striving *forward* toward justice. You must see there are always fresh hatreds to sow; stop perpetuating

[26] "A man is the whole encyclopedia of facts. The creation of a thousand forests is in one acorn, and Egypt, Greece, Rome, Gaul, Britain, America, lie folded already in the first man. Epoch after epoch, camp, kingdom, empire, republic, democracy, are merely the application of his manifold spirit to the manifold world." *-R.W. Emerson*

[27] "I am of old and young, of the foolish as much as the wise,/Regardless of others, ever regardful of others,/Maternal as well as paternal, a child as well as a man,/Stuffed with the stuff that is coarse, and stuffed with the stuff that is fine... A learner with the simplest, a teacher of the thoughtfulest,/A novice beginning experient of myriads of seasons/Of every hue and trade and rank, of every caste and religion/Not merely of the New World but of Africa Europe or Asia.... a wandering savage,/A farmer, mechanic, or artist.... a gentleman, sailor, lover or quaker,/A prisoner, fancy-man, rowdy, lawyer, physician or priest." *-W. Whitman*

resentment! We teach unity across once impenetrable barriers: we help humans *see humans—Americans see Americans.*

"If you really care about the future, what of the environment?" Liberals recall a bipartisan consensus which stood for the voiceless creatures charged to our care—which passed groundbreaking legislation as a model to the world.[28] Does progressivism champion *species preservation*, trees, or ecological wonders? Your advocacy is for centralized power; your *passion* is for phantom bureaucracy. You bleed Red not green.

You subvert environmentalism with nonsensical associations. A liberal wonders: how dire is climate catastrophe if *the world ends* each time a child's nonconforming pronoun is ignored? You have taught that *science is perspective*; you have desecrated a holy mandate for public health and biological preservation by intertwining conservation with politicized "science" and your enlargements of government in the social sphere.

[28] Peter long believed that the greatest forward-thinking achievement of any democratic people, unsurpassed in leadership, humility, and scope of vision, was the passage of the Endangered Species Act and the Clean Air Act. (LW)

Do you not comprehend? You piggyback environmentalism to exercise your lust for control. Earth's challenges *require globally and federally coordinated responses*! But, rather than engage in the persuasion required to legislate, you have removed environmentalism from the public forum through flimsy reinterpretations of outdated law. The current EPA regulatory regime targeting greenhouse gas emissions derives its authority from statutes which are 40 years old—passed in complete ignorance of climate shifts. Please consider: administrators can always butcher dictionary definitions in the pursuit of policy-making, but bad faith reinterpretations of mismatched statutes link action on climate change to authoritarianism—both in practice and in the citizen consciousness. In a democracy, agents of change must *make better arguments*, not circumvent legislation.

Environmental regulation, an imperative of responsibility and interconnectedness, is properly viewed as a *necessary* exception to our system of limited sovereignty. Federal powers are expanded to combat problems unaccounted for by any previous political designs.[29]

The prevention of *irreparable* biological harm justifies a revised separation of powers and intrusions into private conduct.[30]

There is *no similar authorization* for such structural alterations in the ever evolving and imminently correctable social arena. Ecological issues are supremely unique; there is no potential for future democratic redress of environmental destructions. To go extinct is to be gone forever. Nationalists care deeply for our biospheric heritage and the protection of natural resources; any nation which seeks to lead must prioritize scientific exploration and informed policy. We fail to understand why in voting for action against climate change we have been forced to consider the regulation or use of gendered bathrooms.

---

[29] "Modern technology has introduced actions of such novel scale, objects, and consequences that the framework of former ethics can no longer contain them...the nature of human action has *de facto* changed... an object of an entirely new order—no less than the whole biosphere of the planet—has been added to what we must be responsible for because of our power over it." -*H. Jonas*

[30] "Must our law be so rigid and our procedural concepts so inflexible that we render ourselves helpless when the existing methods and the traditional concepts do not quite fit and do not prove to be entirely adequate for new issues?" -*J. Blackmun*

People evolve toward new conventions through democratic discourse. Nationalists believe in adaptation; *they welcome social activism*. But, by imposing agendas through administrative law and judicial fiat, progressives neglect the *work of social change*. A free society can be convinced to legislate against hate: through debate the people learn new acceptances and purge themselves of fear. A *ruled society* embraces bigoted impulses as the only permissible rebellion against its masters. Man loathes the loss of empowerment more than the substance of any edict.

Law is a blunt instrument that oversimplifies infinite individual circumstances, political pressures, and moral theories into a basic code applicable to all. The "fairness" of law is debatable no matter its author; law is made "just" *by the citizen's right* to sculpt its demands. Nationalists compose a republic, not a mess of aliens united only through bondage. Here, the people rule![31]

[31] "It is, I believe, a matter of sensibility. It involves our assumptions, imagination, and... attitudes toward the political energy of ordinary people. For that is the kernel of democracy, of a regime in which offices are open to ordinary citizens and in which ordinary people are allowed, and even expected, to act collectively to influence, and even control, the government. After all, democracy—its aspirations, its operation, its dangers—is what, most fundamentally, our Constitution is *about*." -R. Parker

The accusations which call nationalism a creed of racial or gender-based exclusion are ridiculous, lazy, stupid, condescending, dismissive, insidious, destructive, obnoxious..., and will be dispatched with little discussion.

Liberals refuse to infantilize or dismiss female choice with lies about social conditioning. Progressives see a woman as something to be led, a thing so delicate it can only bow to cultural expectations. By seeing no strength or potential for uncoerced decisions, they call female autonomy impossible. Progressives then wish to be the kinder overlord who supplants one oppressive set of mandates with their own. Liberals do not reject femininity or masculinity; professional ambition or domesticity; our women are citizens. We refuse to batter either gender into compliance with equivalent social statistics or vocational aesthetics. *No data can qualify female advancement*; individual women decide what it means to advance.

"What of the nationalists' growing desire to stem the immigration of foreign peoples and cultures?" We lament this unfortunate but necessary response to progressivism.

Progressives have made America unworthy of welcoming anyone. The sacred words of modernity have long been "Come to America, *Become American*". Nationalists celebrate all peoples as capable of *learning liberty and practicing self-governance*. Progressives believe that new additions are inferior to the task of the American experiment; their racism is shameful. They have stolen that birthright from the world.

They shout that, but for progressivism, bigotry and economic injustice erect permanent barriers to immigrant success. These characterizations degrade the generational undertaking to change, to improve, and to embrace American society and citizenship. Progressives besmirch the dignity of new Americans by proclaiming that the only path to prosperity is through fealty to progressive governance. Progressives would deprive immigrants of the greatest gifts: the struggle to assimilate, the struggle to overcome, and the struggle to join and mold the fabric of American identity.

Immigrants *remain* the revitalizing force which ever renews American ambition, adaptation, resilience, and optimism. Progressives teach that immigrants who embrace our society are acquiescing to racism, that to be molded or to love *their new country* is to slavishly bow to a masters' culture. By trying to keep immigrants—and a variety of domestic ethnicities—foreign, progressivism perpetuates the color line; the nationalist believes America can bridge it.[32]

"What about our duties to refugees?" Progressives long to obliterate civil society under the guise of humanitarianism; they hunger for untethered peoples as weapons for the consolidation of our money and political control. Nationalists bear no malice to foreign victims:

---

[32] "I sit with Shakespeare, and he winces not... From out of the caves of evening that swing between the strong-limbed Earth and the tracery of stars, I summon Aristotle and Aurelius and what soul I will, and they come all graciously with no scorn nor condescension. So, wed with Truth, I dwell above the veil. Is this the life you grudge us, O knightly America ... Are you so afraid lest peering from this high Pisgah, between Philistine and Amalekite, we sight the Promised Land?" -*W.E.B. Du Bois*

while progressivism exists we fear that new Americans will be taught hatred, taught dependency, and taught destruction.

Nationalism's border policy expresses its rejection of progressivism's corrosive influence. We do not detest immigrants; we want no more progressives. We reject samaritan arguments that sacrifice liberty or safety.

We have shown that to combat progressivism's legacy of eroding free democracy, citizen happiness, and national cohesion, liberals must coalesce around a message with the power to wipe that stain from societal imagination; subject to tremendous controls, they must fight for reasoning, for unity, and for joy.

The nationalist is the vessel by which this will be accomplished. The future entails radical alterations to the role of government and to our understandings of the proper spheres in which popular will and expert opinion should exert authority. New technologies, mass migrations, and environmental preservation test institutional capabilities. The *character* of the people who meet these challenges is of paramount importance. Nationalism rejects tyranny as it rejects madness and chaos; the future cannot be met by managers alone. With firmness in the right as God gives us to see the right, it will be overcome by Americans—by a united people each of whom possess the ability to discern the merits and direction of mankind.

There will be pain as the people are roused from the mistakes and path dependencies which they have been taught to tolerate as permanent. The following measures start that journey: they will be superseded and refined as the cleverness of lawyers renders them ineffective:

1. Mandatory completion of public primary and secondary education, or 3 years of military service.[33]

2. Mandatory religious education in any sect of a major religion chosen by parents;[34] Mandatory financial and

---

[33] The true deleterious consequences of wealth inequality are the escape from social comingling and lack of political seriousness endemic to the affluent—they have "no skin in the game" or investment in public institutions. Their willingness to entertain and endorse the increasing absurdity of progressivism stems from the boredom and ennui which often accompanies moneyed detachment from the immediate needs of society. (LW)

[34] We do not establish or advance any religion nor foresee any excessive state

economic literacy training, study of American civics, *its intellectual forerunners*, constitutional separation of powers, and administrative law taught throughout primary and secondary schooling. A criminal ban on personal internet access for minors.[35]

3. The division of higher education into job training institutes, or arts and science research universities; modification of vocational curriculum to admit all new practitioners to any profession by age 21; businesses or institutions which claim to require additional training of junior employees must provide it as part of salaried duties; ban on the creation of additional degrees or certifications. A constitutional amendment barring government interference or "aid" in the market for education.[36]

---

entanglements with religion; rather this measure primarily serves *a secular purpose*: that of tutoring our citizenry toward becoming more aware, more interesting, and more capable of abstract thought and conviction. (LW)

[35] "A young thing can't judge what is hidden sense and what is not; but what he takes into his opinions at that age has a tendency to become hard to eradicate and unchangeable. Perhaps it's for this reason that we must do everything to insure that what they hear first, with respect to virtue, be the finest told tales for them to hear." -*Plato*

4. A hard cap—20% of the eligible population—on the amount of student seats available at research universities, split 85/15 between natural sciences and humanities.[37]

5. Tax incentives for businesses to provide time off to employees who participate in political associations, elected offices, or community activism.[38]

6. Mandatory term limits of elected representatives; repeal of the 17th amendment; a constitutional amendment

---

[36] Measures three and four both confront what has happened to the modern university. An enlightenment era embodiment of the quest for truth and knowledge has been replaced with corporate profit centers which at best fail completely in their mandate to educate. The captured market for meaningless credentials is one of the most significant barriers to class advancement or integration, a vulgar tool of redistributionist oppression, and a monopoly-protecting choke on dynamism and maturity. The cowardly responses to campus turmoil are no mystery: student checks still cash regardless of how they act or whether they learn to think. (LW)

[37] "The ceaseless, senseless demand for original scholarship in a number of fields, where only erudition is now possible, has led either to sheer irrelevancy, the famous knowing of more and more about less and less, or to the development of a pseudo-scholarship which actually destroys its object." - *H. Arendt* (LW)

[38] "The task of the social power will... constantly increase, and its very efforts will make it vaster each day. The more it puts itself in place of associations, the more particular persons, losing the idea of associating with each other, will need it to come to their aid: these are causes and effects that generate each other without rest. Will the public administration in the end direct all the industries for which an isolated citizen cannot suffice?...In order that men remain civilized or become so, the art of associating must be developed and perfected among them in the same ratio as equality of conditions increases." - *A. Tocqueville*

capping nondiscretionary federal spending at 40% of the yearly budget regardless of balance or imbalance.[39]

7. Mandatory Congressional reassessments and reauthorization votes on all legislation which delegates authority to agency actors, every 3 years; Constitutional amendment to limit the legality of delegations to agencies solely to scientific and *quantifiable matters* of public health, environmentalism, and consumer safety.[40]

8. *Any policy...* which aims to *gain control* over the inflow of immigrants; permitted amounts based on connections to domestic families and tangible educational or employment opportunities; deportation of aliens convicted of crimes; accelerated paths to citizenship for

---

[39] Peter was an anti-dogmatist; democracy is good, checks on democracy are good—democracy-destroying obligations which make responsive or innovative policy impossible are not so good. (LW)

[40] "The power of an administrative agency to administer a congressionally created ...program necessarily requires the formulation of policy and the making of rules to fill any gap left, implicitly or explicitly, by Congress." *Morton v. Ruiz*, 415 U.S. 199, (1974)... Such legislative regulations are given controlling weight unless they are arbitrary, capricious, or manifestly contrary to the statute. Sometimes the legislative delegation to an agency on a particular question is implicit rather than explicit." -*J. Stevens*

resident aliens based on completion of standard civics education or military service.[41]

9. The pursuit of a global convention to *define* and ban "thinking" artificial intelligences and to control the pathways of human genetic modifications.[42]

10. The pursuit of a national and global series of initiatives and treaties, with draconian enforcement mechanisms, to legally designate half the world's surface land and seas as protected biosphere; the creation and funding of an international registry and depository charged with collecting the DNA of every known species.[43]

---

[41] "We throw open our city to the world, and never by alien acts exclude foreigners from any opportunity of learning or observing, although…the enemy may occasionally profit by our liberality; [we trust] less in system and policy than to the native spirit of our citizens…" -*Thucydides*

[42] "One Law for the Lion & Ox is Oppression". -*W. Blake.* The definition of justice subscribed to by higher or different intelligences may not comport with our own. See e.g., whales and elephants relationships to man. Until the causal dynamics between DNA and specific allelic expressions or protein interconnectivities are *fully* understood safeguards should be clear and precautionary. (LW)

[43] "The well-taught philosophic mind/To all compassion gives;/Casts round the world an equal eye,/And feels for all that lives./If mind, as ancient sages taught,/A never dying flame,/Still shifts thro' matter's varying forms,/In every form the same,/Beware, lest in the worm you crush/A brother's soul you find;/And tremble lest thy luckless hand/Dislodge a kindred mind./Or, if this transient gleam of day/Be all of life we share,/Let pity plead within thy breast,/That little all to spare." -*A.L. Aikin* (LW)

Nationalists fight for their faith: the reasoning of the average person *must and can* continuously be brought to a level of capability and reflection which allows for informed civic action. They see the folly of progressive obsessions; ask a newly diagnosed cancer patient whether social planning can ever fully equalize power or make life *fair*. Man's greatest strength and rightful mission is the development of informed judgment and spiritual gentillesse regardless of circumstance or station.[44]

Nationalism will replace today's distractions with a shared American identity. You shall no longer crucify us upon a cross of progressivism's nocebo effect. A massive nation will always provide examples to support any regressive theory; somewhere there is a 12 year old on a message board. Nationalists pay no attention to petty anomalies. Our people are a nation more just, more diverse—yet more emblematic of universal brotherhood—than any yet seen. We

---

[44]   "We do not hold, as the many do, that preservation and mere existence are what is most honorable for human beings; what is most honorable is for them to become as excellent as possible and to remain so for as long a time as they may exist." *-Plato*

will not sacrifice our rights; we will not accept terrorism in our daily existence as privacy and liberty vanish. We condemn the globalists who look abroad in a failed attempt to exonerate their hidden guilt— the knowledge that their own children are less free, less prosperous, and less capable than they were.

In place of progressivism we will have a common society, an educated society, a society inhabited by equal political animals. Nationalism provides the communal cause—the bulwark against devolving into a land of ignorant armies clashing in darkness!

Chapter III. Misguided Patriots

1. Incubating Nationalists

A. Senile Leftists

Before concepts like "rebellion", "speaking truth to power", and "self-expression" became merely the most efficient ways to sell merchandise, there were those who felt that America's majority culture had failed to honor its avowed noble ideals. In reaction to what they saw as hypocrisy, several generations aspired to stand apart from a rotten "normal" which preached freedom and justice while engaging in bigotry, unjust war, and repression. Frustrated but hopeful, they sought to honor their nations foundational promises, protest intolerance, and defend the basic rights of all citizens.

The hippies, the beatniks, the civil rights activists, the folk musicians—despite what they may believe about themselves—were not revolutionaries; they instead hoped to banish false congregants

74

from the American temple. They did not reject the traditional creed but rather longed to see it fully realized and practiced; in their hearts, these rebels yearned for a *more rigorous and thorough expression of espoused national values.* A country which speaks of universal equality, religious love, and natural freedoms cannot discriminate, segregate, or disgrace itself by failing to treat all of its members as equal beneficiaries and social partners.

To ensure that this land belonged to every individual citizen they taught love for all peoples as brothers and sisters in a universal family. They rightly understood segregation and identity-based hatred as shame before the entire world and *legislated* against bigotry. Most importantly, they molded the hearts of America's citizenry. Laws are secondary to the cumulative impact of each person's daily desires and actions; the greatest enforcer of anti-discriminatory policy is a loving inclination fostered within a populace. They hugged and kissed a United States of mutual responsibility, tolerance, and charity;[45] this stewardship also led to

---

[45] "Visions! omens! hallucinations! miracles! ecstasies! gone down the American river!/Dreams! adorations! illuminations! religions! the whole boatload of sensitive bullshit!" -*A. Ginsberg*

experiments in social spending with the goal of caring for the disabled and the destitute.

But, the senile leftists have failed to identify and reckon with the creeping progressive reorientation of their once pure dreams. Does today's activism preach fellowship and democratic engagement? Is there a robust civic intercourse replete with appeals to the hearts inner voice of conscience? The senile leftists hear but do not *listen* to progressives; they who once believed that the truest expression of America was found in civil rights, legal egalitarianism, and mutual affection have stood aside as their nation's soul and history have been reinterpreted, as their countrymen have been damned as beyond salvation, as equality has been called impossible without *state intercession* against the oppressor majority. The senile leftists once marched believing love would conquer hate;[46] progressives now throw tantrums calling for the machine gun hand to subdue their opponents.

---

[46] For an alternative viewpoint see Lana Weelhans, The False Recollections of Upper Class Posers; The 1960's Actually Sucked and Destroyed America; see also, Lana Weelhans, You Were Not Involved; Civil Rights Succeeded Independent from Counter-Culture Nonsense.

Cozying up to the new bosses of our society, the senile leftists have shed their distrust of authority; too secure in wealth and status, and too afraid of being labeled "squares", they have abandoned their distaste for hypocrisy, for agents of division, and for oppression masquerading as law.

Most unforgivably, they acquiesced as progressivism delinked human rights from God.[47] In their cowardice they have left behind the *principle source of civil equality and validation for democracy.* Were they even listening? The holy rhetoric and central mission of the last century's most noble triumphs would be castigated as devotional fanaticism by today's "leaders". Progressivism burns down the churches which only decades before served as the wellspring of freedom rising. We ask the senile leftists whether they have forsaken *all* that they once believed. Do you now assert that brute caprice is the only law of the universe? That there is no inner light of love and redemption? That the races cannot live together

[47] "Who gave us the sponge to wipe away the entire horizon? What were we doing when we unchained this earth from its sun? Whither is it moving now? Whither are we moving? Away from all suns? Are we not plunging continually? Backward, sideward, forward, in all directions? Is there still any up or down? Are we not straying as through an infinite nothing? Do we not feel the breath of empty space? Has it not become colder? Is not night continually closing in on us?" -F. Nietzsche

peacefully and in that failure must be controlled for their own safety? If you have abandoned the optimism of your youth, if you have learned the most cynical historical narratives, please... please! Lend a hand by taking your broken hearts elsewhere. Liberals still *work to freely make* the world safe for diversity.[48]

You must choose what you believe about mankind's potential; there is no shortage of evidence to prove or disprove *any* generalization about our capacities for empathy or cruelty. As your false heirs obsessively emphasize the space between us all, nationalists stand ready to receive you back into the fold of those who continue to labor toward *standing* together in glory.

B. The People

Never truly homogenous in needs, region, age, or ambitions, the people are *a projection of the average person.* In any democracy, policy decisions are evaluated by their impact upon this class; politicians court kinship with their ranks and promise to prioritize their economic health.

---

[48] "Tell me love is not lost...without love, day to day,/Insanity is king...without love in a dream/it will never come true" -*R. Hunter*

78

The people affirm that individuals *who work hard and contribute to society,* or the truly in need, have the right to expect economic security, family stability, and access to basic necessities from cradle to grave; a civilized nation must reward *the character and industriousness* of average law-abiding citizens. Like the nationalists, they refuse to allow man to be left behind or exploited by technology or industry; they assert that as innovations and trade alter the paradigms of work, satisfying the basic needs of the people must remain the first priority of any new era. Their demands for dignified wages, humane treatment, access to affordable education, and decent healthcare stem from the righteous conviction that all civic participants deserve fair compensation for their role in upholding social order.

The people suffer the symptoms of upheaval: loss of mobility, stymied access to goods and services, and depleted economic and political power. Progressivism often manipulates their justifiable *fear* of changing circumstances—it is vital that government minds the speed of metamorphosis, uses conscience to reign in markets, and provides a safety net to aid adaptations to change—but, the people must vigilantly purge the *social* scum from their ranks. Progressive disempowerment *prioritizes* control and dependency: it dangles essentials for "free" while making true quality unaffordable and weaponizes envy to grow the federal leviathan at taxpayer expense. Where are the organizers for revolutions in primary education or more creative cultivations of worker elasticity? The people are not covetous progressives, they want what all deserve: the ability for their reasonable toil to provide reasonable comfort.[49]

The pain of *inevitable shifts* in the value of skills, labor, and entire industries is prolonged by political exploitation; the peoples' leadership erects temporary and ineffective hindrances against the dynamism of a changing economy; *most* measures stifle a workers ability to transition between jobs, or aid slivers of vocations at the expense of others, and *always* brutalize and impoverish the dwindling "middle class". Their triumphs too often outlive their

---

[49] "You need to know that it is your duty to rise above the animal plane of existence….to know something about literature and science and art… as long as you are ignorant, as long as you are indifferent, as long as you are apathetic, unorganized and content, you will remain exactly where you are. You will be exploited; you will be degraded, and you will have to beg for a job." *-E.V. Debs*

usefulness and linger on as outdated and inefficient drains on prosperity or antidemocratic burdens on future generations.

C. Libertarian Lunatics

Are the people unhappy with low wages' purchasing power, business monopolies, and wealth inequality? What about the exploding costs of healthcare and education, or corrupt politicians' subservience to moneyed interests? One seldom meets more devout adherents to a quasi-religious doctrine than the libertarian lunatics and their free market solutions.

And they are so often prescient. Markets cannot be restrained for long; the millions of independent decisions made by a population eventually dictate prices. Stifling the outcomes of free choices entrenches wealth and power while impoverishing the pockets of society that bear the unavoidable costs. Shortages in doctors and healthcare, cartel restrictions of access to legal services, unequal distributions of the benefits of global trade, extreme boom and bust cycles, unemployable workers, bankrupt municipalities, general feelings of unpleasantness, student loan debt—all are *mostly* explainable by regulatory hurdles and rent-seeking corruptions. Our present generation's "great" social insurance program was an overt scam designed to force the last of the self-sufficient non-rich onto welfare, government's inability to allocate resources has conscripted the young in service to the upkeep of unsustainable promises, and a rudimentary understanding of capital markets dispels any notion of a wealthy class destroying productivity by hoarding money.

Libertarian Lunatics understand that no one can fathom entire systems of economic interactions; planners inevitably do not see the ways their distortions reverberate. The creativity of the people is unparalleled in subverting intrusive designs. Our ruling classes struggle to accept that high standardized test scores have not immunized them from a mere pretense of knowledge regarding the best ways to serve the needs of a nation.

Herein lies an organic critique of libertarian lunatics; mankind's ignorance of remote economic causes *extends even further* into unquantifiable realms.[50] Awareness of extreme wealth inequality, the

[50]   "…in the study of such complex phenomena as the market, which depend on

initial allocations of chance advantages, and unfair perceptions of secondary status impose spiritual detriments for which no model or theory can fully account. Free markets incontrovertibly lower costs and enhance shared material prosperity, but so what? Economic thinkers, centuries behind real thinkers, love saying people are not fully rational; a society of moguls and paupers will not endure via a shared five cent reduction in the price of milk.

All causes give way to circumstances; Libertarian Lunatics can resemble progressives in their inability to abandon stubborn Utopianism. A fatal conceit *may* be the conviction that any polity blessed with healthy political engagement should or *could* ever sustain a prolonged laissez-faire with regard to every situation faced. America *ratified* the 16th amendment; battles over the Federal Reserve Bank were fought and *settled*; no government or nation could exist which permitted *all* private contracts to trump the democratic mandates of public policy.

---

the actions of many individuals, all the circumstances which will determine the outcome of a process... will hardly ever be fully known or measurable....in the social sciences often that is treated as important which happens to be accessible to measurement." -*F. Hayek*

In common with large corporate entities, government is defined by waste and incompetence. Yet, it remains a valuable source of good. Science should not advance solely in directions lighted by the profit-motive, many public health measures must be prophylactic, and some ecological sustentation transcends monetary value. The advanced state of research guarantees that future breakthroughs will be both collaborative and expensive. Consider all the civilizational successes—in stability, in priorities, in the marshalling of talent—which allow science to progress *for the public benefit.*

Although talk of market failures is usually politicized nonsense, people are *truly incapable* of having full information regarding the choices presented by technology. We may soon live on the moon or mars and beyond; liberals have decided that man is the thing worth sending—that a soul exists—that we must face and *define* the contours of technological aids versus replacements. Before manipulating the genome to liberate us from *some* of nature's cruelties, we must enshrine principles that would protect *you* from elimination once the super "humans" are born.

We suspect that the youngest, more *self-interest*ed, libertarian lunatics have never known fear or have yet to learn of pain, desperation, infirmity, or dependence in ways that would properly frame how little theory matters to individuals. A hungry new born does not care how well people could live in 20 years if the government would only stop inadvertently subsidizing its parents' industry today. Economics is not a science; it is a tool used in persuasion and limited explanation. Like any tool, its utility is dependent on the goals and judgments of its wielder.

Libertarian Lunatics represent themselves best when focused on the alleviation of suffering and the preservation of liberty.[51] Their insights and creativity often solve and demonstrate the simplicity of seemingly complex problems. Democratic politics is defined by competing interests and the moral hazard they inevitably create;

[51] "…there can be no doubt that some minimum of food, shelter, and clothing, sufficient to preserve health and the capacity to work, can be assured to everybody… the case for the state's helping to organize a comprehensive system of social insurance is very strong…there is no incompatibility in principle between the state's providing greater security in this way and the preservation of individual freedom." -*F. Hayek*

libertarian lunatics are most persuasive when arguing from honest ethical concern and a deeply felt sense of duty towards their nation.

2. True Believers

As the only people who realize that *faith in free choice of the will is a prerequisite for the existence of political liberty*, the true believers know that reason—the viceroy of God within us—is called upon to express and defend humanity's glimpses of divine wisdom. Accepting eternal truth as the only boundless reservoir of authority, they educate mankind's practical judgment to the height of its imperfect capabilities.[52]

The true believers live by the obvious principle that the soul requires training. There is no assurance that man will naturally choose the path that does not stray; without correct moral guidance, individuals and nations waste away while courting the lowest elements of their nature. The *American faithful* historically embody the belief that no

---

[52] "…there is in us the knowledge of certain general principles, but not proper knowledge of each single truth…on the part of the practical reason man has a natural participation of the eternal law, according to certain general principles, but not as regards the particular determination of individual cases, which are, however, contained in the eternal law [Hence the necessity that human reason proceed to certain particular sanctions of law.]" -*T. Aquinas*

matter the form taken by God's children—no matter what name or title they present—all are endowed with the spirit of creation.[53]

The national mosaic of faiths coexist and preserve a government which respects the dual-citizenry of religious adherents. The wise devotee is quick to acknowledge the frailty of worldly certitude and so charges the state with humility. True believers know that religious belief *and practice* are the animating foundations of American identity; government exists to *preserve* these freedoms. True believers *affirm* that truth triumphs over falsehood through the free and open exchange of ideas between peoples.

In that spirit we say unto you that America is the highest corporeal representation of your convictions. Our national heritage, a diverse society of friends, has subsumed and altered all creeds for the better. Let us proclaim our mysterious faith: religious patriots are, knowingly or otherwise, *more Americans* than they are strict

[53] "Wee desire... not to judge least we be judged, neither to condemn least we be condemned, but rather let every man stand or fall to his own Master. Wee are bounde by the law to do good unto all men... the powers of this world can neither attach us, neither excuse us, for if God justifye who can condemn and if God condemn there is none can justifye." -*F. Remonstrance*

members of their respective creeds—in that contradiction is the purest union of their beliefs. The unique forces of various unwritten American dogma have subtly changed or reinterpreted scripture and its applied practices to comport with national identity.[54]

And that canon is in danger. As citizenship in a bad city tempts you to recoil from public life, we implore you—remain stalwart, do not withdraw from the American project! The forces beyond your control which mold man's essence have risen in intensity and reach. As they slither into all enclaves and conquer vulnerable minds, resignation is not a safe option. You must continue to impress virtue upon your children *and also* upon the national culture and legal regime. No constitutional structures will defend you from the ignominious manipulations perpetrated by unjust rulers; necessity compels you to care for the governance and soul of your nation. Proclaim the difference between freedom and licentiousness; that autonomy is possible only through rigor and mastery of self; that pseudo-intellectual pyrotechnics are pathetic substitutes for

---

[54] See Lana Weelhans; "In Bed with Queequeg; God's Love for Blasphemy in the Name of Brotherhood". (LW)

revelation. As the people grow more fierce and wild, true believers must actively hear and channel God's call.

3. Constitutional Nerds

Constitutional nerds provide an elegant solution to the problems of partisan failures to communicate: The Constitution, The Declaration of Independence, and centuries of legal decisions tell us who we are as a people—there is no American identity separate from this jurisprudence. Religion, race, gender, and class are secondary considerations; constitutional authority is what all cite for validation of their political arguments or social aspirations; in discourse on rights, it is the Constitution all seek to expound.

In a world in which truth and justice live and die via the appropriate use of commas or italicization—where entire careers are forged by the interpretation of a single sentence—constitutional nerds have developed their own creation myths complete with several falls and multiple schisms. In the beginning there was the founding generation who created the heavens and The Constitution; injustice and Civil War modified The Constitution in substantial ways transforming America into a completely different legal nation. Then, revealing that both *the North and the South lost the war to the federal bench*, judges went to work enlarging the carefully circumscribed powers of the federal government... or they integrated dispersed powers into a workable government... or relied upon the mystery of human life to do whatever they wanted.

Constitutional nerds, *for the most part*, oppose judicial activism; an unelected body should not hinder the people's democratic influence. But, *the Supreme Court is the defender of fundamental rights* against state or federal legislation. The protections of the Bill of Rights are shielded from abridgement by state or federal governments, but political leanings then influence how many *other* rights, judicially created ... or discovered, which may... or may not... comport with our nation's history and traditions, a constitutional nerd will acknowledge as fundamental.[55] They believe it is the duty of judges

[55] Over time the entire Bill of Rights has been incorporated into the due process clause of the 14th amendment and thus applies against state governments. The predominant tension in this jurisprudence boils down to which rights are "higher" or "constitutionally protected" and therefore insulated from state democratic process, and who gets to decide that question. This is best understood by way of example: *Roe v. Wade* establishes a fundamental right to abortion. Is this a pure judicial creation? Or is due process an open ended term subject to changing times? Should history and tradition limit how open-ended? Which traditions? And who has the right to answer these questions? An unelected court? The legislature? The people? If there is mass

to say what the law is, not what it should be; shame on judges who, hoping their opinions will be recited, abandon writing analytically in favor of spouting juvenile clichés.

Law forcibly distills the knowledge, beliefs, and hopes of all human endeavors into meaningful and sometimes hilarious simplicity... or jargon... interpreted by brilliant, flawed, and obsessive citizens. Constitutional nerds have some good natured questions: Is anything free from the economic tendrils of the commerce clause? How does equal protection give judges magical powers to interpolate animus into the hearts of legislators? Why is the constitution commercially neutral but a social bohemian? How could a government of enumerated powers have the right to regulate the externalities of non-conduct? If a tax is not a tax but also is a tax, at what point are

---

disagreement about whether a right enshrined is "higher" is that an argument for why courts should leave the issue to democracy, or *exactly the reason* courts are charged with guarding the rights of the vulnerable? The Bill of Rights is bound up in our foundation through specific amendments. Beyond them, fundamental rights creation risks politicizing law. Can law be apolitical? Should it be? Gun rights cases have proven that even protections listed in The Bill of Rights require some level of judicial defining. Reasonable minds disagree; Constitutional law *may* offer clear rules, or comprise a suicide pact, or merely exist as the agreed upon language and doctrine one must at least pretend to care about in advancing a cause; society functions when everyone respects the rules of the game. Except when there is a higher game; are all higher games created equal? (LW)

judicial rewrites of law recklessly irresponsible? Can anyone safely define the hallmarks of corruption from corporate political speech in a way that would not logically devolve into book burning? What kind of agency is the SEC? Do words have meaning?[56]

Constitutional nerds worry that our legal regime has erased the republic; that the majority of meaningful issues, matters the people should rightfully decide, are now resolved by the judiciary or the administrative state. Legislative gridlock favors and rewards this devolution; lawmakers can avoid a controversial record by skirting their duties knowing that the other branches of government will take action free from democratic accountability. Representatives may soon campaign and legislate to abolish suffering itself, with the definition of suffering and the law's implementation to be articulated and carried out by the CFPB.

---

[56]   No, but the only substantial effect that would come from limiting the commerce clause is a plethora of necessary and proper expansions; It shouldn't, but The Supreme Court is "not final because [it is] infallible, but [it is] infallible only because [it is] final"; Herbert Spencer's Social Statistics are not as satisfying or as sexy as penumbras of rights; *It never should*; Answered in the asking; Peak political absurdity is achieved when quasi-Marxist lawyers cite the fiduciary duties of corporate officers to maximize shareholder value as a way of supporting government regulation of speech; No one knows and no one wants to know; *Id..* (LW)

Some constitutional nerds, in an effort to impose clear standards and democratic processes, proclaim that the original meaning of The Constitution is both ascertainable and authoritative. Others— acknowledging that history, common law evolution, and executive branch transformations have permanently altered the legal regime— focus on faithful adherence to statutory texts as a way of preserving judicial restraint.

Unfortunately, constitutional nerds are priests speaking Latin to a congregation that has not read the holy text. *Liberty is first and foremost a taste* which must be carefully acquired; no paper barrier can liberate an ignorant people or endure against decline. Most citizens define "unconstitutional" as whatever they do not like; constitutional nerds face the classical impotence of all gentle-minded republicans living in a dying republic. Doctrinal mastery is a slim comfort against the awareness that *severe restorative actions may likely backfire* and further speed our Augustinian transformation. To see only a limited choice between impotence and extremism is a painful temptation.[57]

No people can be expected to stand firmly by a governing document they themselves have not studied, whose language they do not fluently speak. Constitutional nerds are not the primary driving force of social events; it is firstly *the people's faith and desires* that are then later adopted and applied through the machinations of constitutional nerds.

We caution against the mad idolatry of service to technicalities at the expense of citizen education and participation in American institutions. Our modern legal regime is a monumental achievement; the vast majority of Supreme Court decisions are unanimous and the controversy around rare disagreements is magnified by intense focus and political pressures. Complete legal certainty is a Sisyphean pursuit; our laws' contradictions better approach justice than any foolish consistency could.[58] The meaning of freedom may be found

---

[57] "Between the acting of a dreadful thing/And the first motion, all the interim is/Like a phantasma, or a hideous dream:/The Genius and the mortal instruments/Are then in council; and the state of man,/Like to a little kingdom, suffers then/The nature of an insurrection." -*W. Shakespeare*

[58] "Certainty generally is illusion and repose is not the destiny of man" -*O.W. Holmes*

in how well citizens can learn to understand and engage with the semi-invisible legal structures which influence their lives. By teaching democracy and discretion you preserve the fragments of a constitutional republic shored against further ruin. Constitutional nerds: continue to struggle valiantly, but keep your sense of humor!

Chapter IV. Immediate Goals of the Nationalist Political Movement.

The preceding chapters have made clear that the unifying force of nationalism is needed to enliven the dormant wisdom *and strength* of America's scattered liberal population.

The nationalists work to elevate liberal passions to the forefront of social consciousness. Despite the progressives' will to self-negation or their attempts to bury politics under layers of arbitrarily "neutral" governing structures, human judgment remains the final arbiter of mankind's affairs—liberals work to *nurture and grow man's reasoning faculties*, not bypass them. Nationalism is the conviction through which citizens may reach and express their fullest potential. The crafting of legal regimes and a moral order—mandates which no ideology can avoid—should rightfully aim for an abundance of human concord and advancement, civic freedom and responsibility, and personal joy.

In combating identity distractions the nationalists educate progressives: *every* reflective person feels alienated and abused by forces beyond their control; the measure of a thriving society is whether it converts these feelings of loneliness into rage and mass resentment or into empathy for the shared experiences of fellow countrymen.

To the flat-headed syllogists they proclaim that a thimble full of *honorable taste is worth more than entire oceans of corrupt erudition*; the earnest practice or profanation of universality, of equality before the law, and of faith in reasoning is easily recognized.

Nationalists will teach liberals to identify the ultimate obliterating goals of progressivism. The day may come when Americans abandon the hope for a *diverse and free* polity, and self-segregate locally or among the stars; man may choose self-modification to such an extent that all modern concerns will be shed as merely the first chapters in the spawning of a higher, synthesized, organism. But, down to the final seconds in which *human imperatives and human dreams claim primacy over this world*, liberalism represents the noblest expression of Man's nature and capacities for justice.

Nationalists do not give in to the progressive desire to erase *human development* as the highest end and measure of a political system's success. Until we choose, or suffer, an as yet uncertain point of departure from our primal condition—an evolution which leaves all human wisdom and identity behind—love, yearning, freedom, *emotions*, markets, science, cogitation, common sense, and faith will drive man's destiny.

Nationalists reinforce prosperity by combating and replacing the progressive disintegrations of all public institutions. They orchestrate a reclamation of American cultural and political expression—the universities, the courts, the arts, news, media, government, and the minds and hearts of American citizenry will no longer suffer progressive corrosions.[59]

In short, nationalists know that progressivism is incompatible with liberalism, incompatible with thriving, and incompatible with bliss.

[59] "A new world/is only a new mind." -*W.C. Williams*

They reject linguistic dissimulations or bad faith accounting for bias—democracies are rightfully led by the reasoning of the people—*the caliber* of the American citizen is their utmost priority.

Finally, they are proud to sing that America is the jewel of all past human endeavor—*if mankind is to have a future the American is that future!*

Nationalists refuse to bow their heads in shame. They no longer grimace in toleration of the calculated destructions wrought by progressive hatred; they seek union with all peoples except those with no love in their souls. Let the bitter beneficiaries of progressive victories be warned and triggered; the nationalists have nothing to lose but misery. They have a nation to set free.

Patriots of America, Crown Thy Good with Brotherhood!

(This day we are jetting the stuff of far more arrogant republics!)

Appendix

Cover Pages

1. The structure and wording of the back cover intentionally mimics the back cover of Marx, Karl and Frederick Engels, *The Communist Manifesto*, ed. and trans. Andrea Gouveia (CreateSpace Independent Publishing Platform, 2016).

2. "The imitator . . . not serious" (p. 3)
    Plato, *The Republic of Plato: Second Edition*, trans. Allan Bloom (New York: Basic Books, 1968), 285.

3. "all nature . . . becomes art" (p. 3)
    Nietzsche, Friedrich, *Gay Science*, trans. Walter Kaufman (New York: Random House, 1974), 303.

4. "Indeed, it . . . things themselves" (p. 4)
    Shakespeare, William, *Julius Caesar*, Act I, Scene 3.

5. "You are . . . killed me" (p. 4)
    Crosby, Stills & Nash, "You Don't Have To Cry", *Crosby, Stills & Nash*, 1969.

Foreword

1. "the intellect . . . to breathe" (p. 7, n.1)
    Wolfe, Virginia, *Orlando* (New York: Mariner Books, 1973), 156.

2. "truth in . . . of illusion" (p. 8)
    Williams, Tennessee, *The Glass Menagerie*, Scene 1.

3. "I present . . . am dead" (p. 8, n.2)
   Poe, Edgar Allan, *Eureka: A Prose Poem*, (Oxford: Benediction Classics, 2011), Preface.

4. "Each age . . . own books" (p. 9)
   Emerson, Ralph Waldo, "The American Scholar", *The Essential Writings of Ralph Waldo Emerson*, ed. Brooks Atkinson (New York: Random House, 2000), 46.

5. "nothing you . . . isn't known" (p. 9)
   The Beatles, "All You Need is Love", *Magical Mystery Tour*, Capitol Records, 1967.

6. "It may . . . to materialize" (p. 10, n.4)
   Bloom, Allan, *The Closing of The American Mind*, Forward. Saul Bellow (New York, Simon & Schuster, 2012), 15.

7. "Beauty is . . . to know" (p. 13)
   Keats, John, "Ode On A Grecian Urn", 1820.

Preamble

1. The structure of the Preamble and much of the entire work is in reference to *The Communist Manifesto* by Karl Marx and Friedrich Engels (1848).

Chapter I

1. "We shall . . . special line" (p. 19, n.5)
   Ortega y Gasset, José, *The Revolt of The Masses* (New York: W. W. Norton & Co., 1994), 79.

2. "ruling group . . . own advantage" (p. 21, n.6)
   Plato, *The Republic of Plato: Second Edition*, trans. Allan Bloom (New York: Basic Books, 1968), 16.

3. "one fact . . . the other" (p. 21, n.6)
   Marx, Karl and Frederick Engels, *The Communist Manifesto*, ed. and trans. Samuel Moore (Washington Square Press, 1964), 92.

4. *"there are...*a misinterpretation" (p. 22, n.7)
   Nietzche, Friedrich, *The Portable Nietzche*, ed. and trans. Walter
   Kaufmann (Viking Penguin Inc., 1982), 501.

5. The phrase "content of their character" (p. 22) is from Luther
   King, Martin, "I Have a Dream" (speech, Washington D.C.,
   August 28, 1963).

6. "The mode . . . consume themselves" (p.24, n.8)
   Machiavelli, Niccolo, *Discourses on Livy*, ed. and trans.
   Mansfield, C. Harvey (University of Chicago Press, 1998) 190.

7. The phrase "iron cage of [bureaucratization]" (p. 26) and "as a . .
   . of content" (p. 26, n.9) are from Weber, Max, *Law in Economy
   and Society*, ed. Max Rheinstein (Cambridge: Harvard
   University Press, 1954), 321.

8. "The word . . . verbal end" (p. 28, n.10)
   Orwell, George, "Politics and the English Language", 1946.

9. "Dave, this . . . anymore. Goodbye." (p. 31, n.11)
   2001: A Space Odyssey. DVD. Dir. Stanley Kubrick. England:
   Metro-Goldwyn-Mayer, 1968.

10. "To escape . . . the Americans" (p. 32, n.12)
    Tocqueville, Alexis de, *Democracy in America*, trans. Harvey C.
    Mansfield and Delba Winthrop (Chicago: The University of
    Chicago Press, 2000), 403.

11. The phrases, "behold the liberal in its new-born blisses" (p. 32),
    "primal sympathy" (p. 33), and "philosophic mind" (p. 33) are
    from Wordsworth, William, "Ode: Intimations of Immortality
    from Recollections of Early Childhood", 1807.

12. The phrase "points of no return" (p. 36) and "the peaceful . . .
    toward disaster" (p. 36, n. 13) are from to Jonas, Hans, *The
    Imperative of Responsibility* (Chicago: The University of
    Chicago Press, 1984), Preface.

13. "We assert . . . [being excellent]" (p. 37, n.14)
    Aristotle, *The Politics*, trans. Carnes Lord (Chicago: The
    University of Chicago Press, 1984), 217.

14. "Citizens, by . . . local discriminations" (p. 38, n.15)
    Washington, George, "Farewell Address" (September 19, 1796).

15. The phrase "we are just one race here. [*It is American*]" (p. 39) is
    from *Adarand Constructors, Inc. v. Peña*, 515 U.S. 200, 239
    (1995) (Scalia, J., concurring).

16. The phrase "the gorgeous [centralizations], the cloud-capped
    [world trade organizations], the solemn [consumer finance
    protections], the great [federal bureaucracy] itself" (p. 40) and
    "shall dissolve . . . rack behind" (p. 40, n.16) are from
    Shakespeare, William, *The Tempest*, Act IV, Scene 1.

17. The phrase "the power to construct a heaven of hell or hell of
    heaven" (p. 40) is from Milton, John, "Paradise Lost" (1667).

18. The phrase "love's not love" (p. 43) is from Shakespeare,
    William, "Sonnet 116" (1609).

19. "Rumour is . . . jealousies, conjectures" (p. 44, n.19)
    Shakespeare, William, *Henry IV Party II*, Prologue.

20. The phrases "admits no impediments" (p. 45), "an ever-fixed
    mark" (p. 45) and "It is . . . be taken" (p. 45, n.20) are from
    Shakespeare, William, "Sonnet 116" (1609).

21. The phrase "a dying animal that knows not [*why*] it is" (p. 45) is
    in reference to Yeats, William Butler, "Sailing to Byzantium"
    (1928).

22. The phrase "lifts the lamp besides the golden door" (p. 46) is in
    reference to Lazarus, Emma, "The New Colossus" (1883).

Chapter II

1. The phrase "better angels of a liberal nature" (p. 48) is in reference to Lincoln, Abraham, "The First Inaugural Address" (speech, Washington, D.C., March 4, 1861).

2. "Deconstruction is . . . real world" (p. 53, n.21)
    Scalia, Antonin, *A Matter of Interpretation: Federal Courts and the Law* (Princeton: Princeton University Press, 1997), 138.

3. The phrase "single garment of destiny" (p. 53) is from King, Martin Luther, "Letter from a Birmingham Jail" (April 16, 1963).

4. The phrase "terrible resolve" (p. 53) is from Yeats, William Butler, "The Second Coming" (1919).

5. The phrase "people grow like savages" (p. 55) and "Even so . . . our country" (p. 55, n.22) are from Shakespeare, William, *Henry V*, Act V, Scene 2.

6. The phrase "piece of work [that] is man" (p. 56) is from Shakespeare, William, *Hamlet*, Act II, Scene 2.

7. "it seems . . . and force" (p. 56, n.23)
    Hamilton, Alexander, "Federalist No. 1" (1787).

8. The phrase "it feels itself too mighty to [aim] small" (p. 56) is from Dunbar, Paul Lawrence, "Fredrick Douglas" (1895).

9. The term "nudge" (p. 58) and the concepts discussed in n.21 are in reference to Thaler, Richard H. and Cass R. Sunstein, *Nudge* (New York: Penguin Books, 2009).

10. The phrase "finds the faults and genius of all persons in all time periods *within*" (pp. 62-63) and "A man . . . manifold world" (p. 63, n.26) are from Emerson, Ralph Waldo, "On History", *The Essential Writings of Ralph Waldo Emerson*, ed. Brooks Atkinson (New York: Random House, 2000), 113.

11. The term "untranslatable" (p. 63) and "I am . . . or priest" (p. 63 n.27) are from Whitman, Walt, "Song of Myself" (1855).

12. The phrase "imperative of responsibility" and "Modern technology . . . over it" (p. 65-66, n.29) are from Jonas, Hans, *The Imperative of Responsibility* (Chicago: The University of Chicago Press, 1984), 6-7.

13. "Must our . . . new issues" (p. 66, n.30)
Sierra Club v. Morton, 405 U.S. 727, 756 (1972) (Blackmun, J., dissenting)

14. The phrase "Here, the people rule" (p. 68) and "It is . . . is *about*" (p. 68, n.31) are from Parker, Richard, *"Here, the People Rule"* (Cambridge: Harvard University Press, 1994), 4.

15. The phrase "color line" (p. 71) and "I sit . . . Promised Land" (p. 70, n.32) are from Du Bois, W.E.B., *The Souls of Black Folk* (Chicago: Dover Publications 1994), 67.

16. The phrase "firmness in the right as God gives us to see the right" (p. 72) is from Lincoln, Abraham, "Second Inaugural Address" (speech, Washington D.C., March 4, 1865).

17. "A young . . . to hear" (p. 74, n.35)
Plato, *The Republic of Plato: Second Edition*, trans. Allan Bloom (New York: Basic Books, 1968), 56.

18. "The ceaseless . . . its object" (p. 75, n.37)
Arendt, Hannah, *On Violence* (New York: Harcourt, 1970), 29-30.

19. "The task . . . conditions increases" (p. 76, n.38)
Tocqueville, Alexis de, *Democracy in America*, trans. Harvey C. Mansfield and Delba Winthrop (Chicago: The University of Chicago Press, 2000), 491-92.

20. "The power . . . than explicit" (p. 77, n.40)

Chevron, U.S.A., Inc. v. Nat. Res. Def. Council, Inc., 467 U.S. 837, 844 (1984)

21. "We throw . . . our citizens" (p. 77, n.41)
Thucydides, *The Landmark Thucydides: A Comprehensive Guide to the Peloponnesian War*, ed. Robert B. Strassler, trans. Richard Crawley (New York: Free Press, Touchstone, 1998), 113.

22. "One Law . . . is Oppression" (p. 78, n.42)
Blake, William, *The Marriage of Heaven and Hell* (Oxford: Oxford University Press, 1975), xxvii.

23. Measure 10 (p. 78) is an idea from Wilson, E.O., *Half-Earth: Our Planet's Fight for Life* (New York: Liveright, 2016).

24. "The well-taught . . . to spare" (p. 78, n.43)
Aikin, Anna Laetitia, "The Mouse's Petition" (1773).

25. "We do . . . may exist" (p. 79, n.44)
Plato, *The Laws of Plato*, trans. Thomas L. Pangle (Chicago: The University of Chicago Press, 1988), 92.

26. The phrase "You shall no longer crucify us upon a cross of [progressivism's nocebo effect]" (p. 79) is from Bryan, William Jennings, "Cross of Gold" (speech, Chicago, IL, July 9, 1896).

27. The phrase "a land of ignorant armies clashing in darkness" (p. 80) is a reference to Arnold, Matthew, "Dover Beach" (1867).

Chapter III

1. The phrase "[hugged and kissed a] United States" (p. 82) and "Visions! omens! . . . sensitive bullshit!" (p. 83, n.45) are from Ginsberg, Alan, "Howl" (1955).

2. The phrase "hear but do not *listen*" (p. 83) is a reference to Simon and Garfunkel, "The Sound of Silence", *Wednesday Morning (3 A.M.)*, Columbia Records, 1964.

3. "Who gave . . . on us?" (p. 84, n.47)
    Nietzsche, Friedrich, *Gay Science*, trans. Walter Kaufmann (New York: Random House, 1974), 181.

4. The phrase "make the world safe for diversity" (p. 85) is from Kennedy, John F., "Commencement Address at the American University" (speech, Washington, D.C., June 10, 1963).

5. "Tell me . . . come true" (p. 85, n.48)
    The Grateful Dead, "Help on The Way", *Blues for Allah*, Grateful Dead Records, 1975.

6. "You need . . . a job" (p. 88, n.49)
    Debs, Eugene V., "Canton, Ohio" (speech, Canton, OH, June 16, 1918).

7. The phrase "pretense of knowledge" (p. 90) and "in the . . . to measurement" (p. 91, n.50) are from August von Hayek, Friedrich, "The Pretense of Knowledge" (Nobel Prize speech, Stockholm, Sweden, December 10, 1974).

8. "there can . . . individual freedom" (p. 94, n.51)
    August von Hayek, Friedrich, *The Road to Serfdom*, ed. Bruce Caldwell (London: The University of Chicago Press, 2007), 148.

9. The phrase "viceroy of God" (p. 94) is a reference to Donne, John, "Holy Sonnets: Batter my heart, three-person'd God" (1633).

10. "there is . . . of law.]" (p. 95, n.49)
    Aquinas, St. Thomas, *The Political Ideas of St. Thomas Aquinas*, ed. Dino Bigongiari (New York, The Free Press, 1997), 15-16.

11. The phrase "the path that does not stray" (p. 95) is from Alighieri, Dante, *Inferno*, trans. Allen Mandelbaum (New York: Bantam Classics, 1982), 3.

12. The phrase "no matter what name or title they present" (p. 95) and "Wee desire . . . can justifye" (p. 95, n.53) is from "The Flushing Remonstrance" (December 27, 1657).

13. The phrase "more fierce and wild" (p. 98) is from Herbert, George, "The Collar" (1633).

14. The phrase "it is the Constitution all seek to expound" (p. 98) is in reference to *McCulloch v. State of Maryland*, 17 U.S. 316, 407 (1819).

15. The phrase "integrated dispersed powers into a workable government" (p. 99) is from *Youngstown Sheet & Tube Co. v. Sawyer*, 343 U.S. 579, 635 (1952) (Jackson, J., concurring).

16. The phrase "mystery of human life" (p. 99) is in reference to *Planned Parenthood of Se. Pennsylvania v. Casey*, 505 U.S. 833, 851 (1992)

17. Pages 99 through 100 and n.555 summarize doctrine from the following cases: *Roe v. Wade*, 410 U.S. 113 (1973) (abortion), *District of Columbia v. Heller*, 554 U.S. 570 (2008) (gun rights) and *McDonald v. City of Chicago*, 561 U.S. 742 (2010) (gun rights). It also references Justice Benjamin Cardozo's view of incorporation in *Palko v. Connecticut*, 302 U.S. 319 (1937) and the opinions voiced by Justices Felix Frankfurter and Hugo Black in *Adamson v. California*, 332 U.S. 46 (1947) and *Rochin v. California*, 342 U.S. 165 (1952). The phrase "suicide pact" is taken from *Terminiello v. City of Chicago*, 337 U.S. 1, 37 (1949) (Jackson, J., dissenting).

18. The questions on page 101 and the answers in n.56 reference the following cases: *United States v. Lopez*, 514 U.S. 549 (1995) (commerce clause); *Romer v. Evans*, 517 U.S. 620 (1996) (animus); and *Nat'l Fed'n of Indep. Bus. v. Sebelius*, 567 U.S. 519 (2012) (tax). The phrase "externalities of non-conduct" is in reference to Justice Ginsburg's opinion in *Nat'l Fed'n of Indep. Bus. v. Sebelius*, 567 U.S. 519, 589 (2012) (Ginsburg, J., concurring in part and dissenting in part), "not final . . . is final"

is from *Brown v. Allen*, 344 U.S. 443, 540 (1953) (Jackson, J., concurring), "Herbert Spencer's Social Statistics" is from *Lochner v. N.Y.*, 198 U.S. 45, 75 (1905) (Holmes, J., dissenting) and the phrase "penumbras of rights" is from *Griswold v Connecticut*, 381 U.S. 479 (1965). Finally, the phrases "corporate speech" and "hallmarks of corruption" are from *Citizens United v. Fed. Election Comm'n*, 558 U.S. 310 (2010).

19. "Between the . . . an insurrection" (p. 103, n.57)
    Shakespeare, William, *Julius Caesar*, Act II, Scene 1.

20. The phrase "mad idolatry" (p. 104) is from Shakespeare, William, *Troilus and Cressida*, Act II, Scene II.

21. "Certainty generally . . . of man" (p. 104, n.58)
    Oliver Wendell Holmes, "The Path of the Law", 110 *Harv. L. Rev.* 991 (1996-1997): 998.

22. The phrase "fragments of a constitutional republic shored against further ruin" (pp. 104-105) is in reference to Elliot, T.S., "The Waste Land" (1922).

Chapter IV

1. "A new . . . new mind" (p. 108, n.59)
   William, Carlos Williams, "To Daphne and Virginia" (1958).

2. The phrase "Crown Thy Good with Brotherhood" (p. 109)
   Ward, Samuel A., "America the Beautiful" (1910).

3. The phrase "This day [we] are jetting the stuff of far more arrogant republics" is taken from Whitman, Walt, "Song of Myself" (1855).

www.ingramcontent.com/pod-product-compliance
Lightning Source LLC
Chambersburg PA
CBHW070641030426
42337CB00020B/4108